2014 << addison karl >> 2015

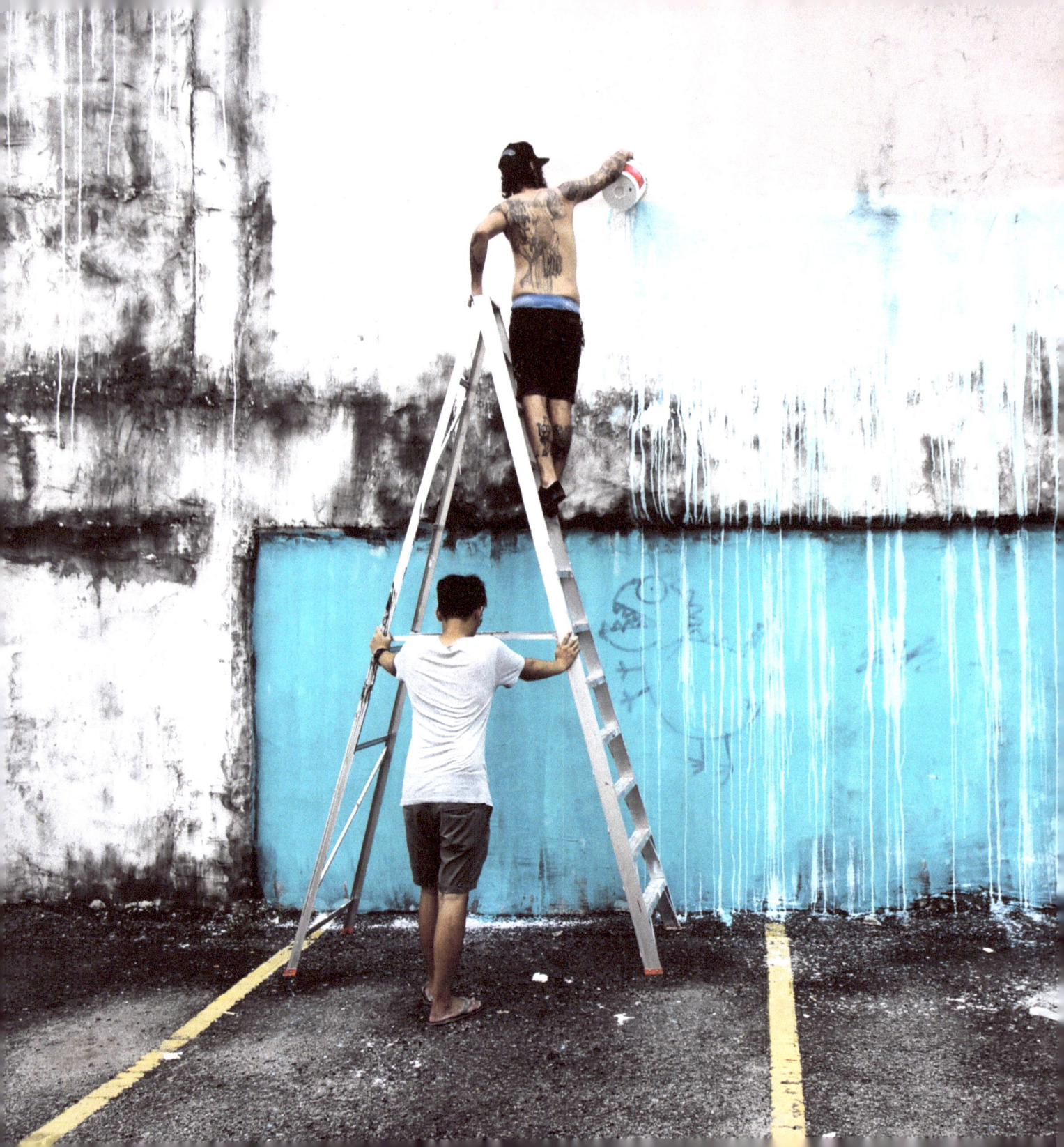

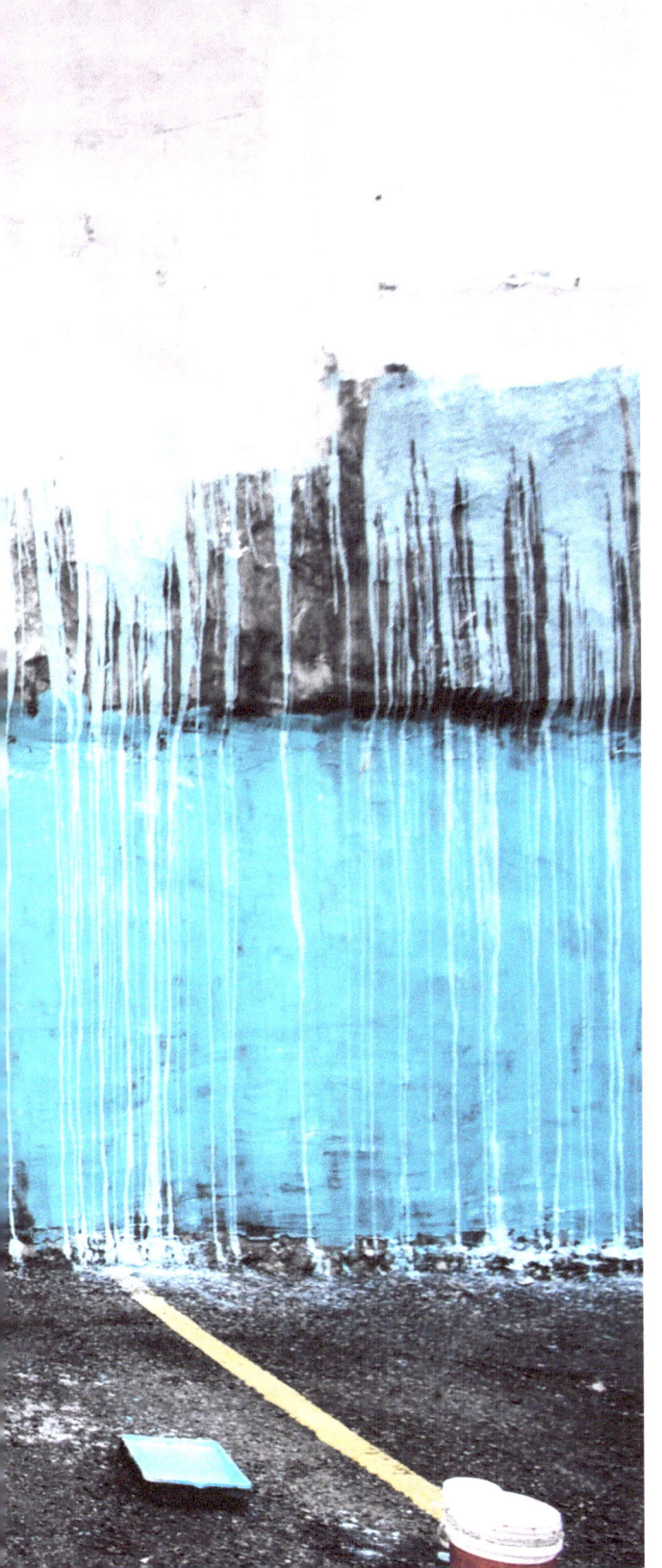

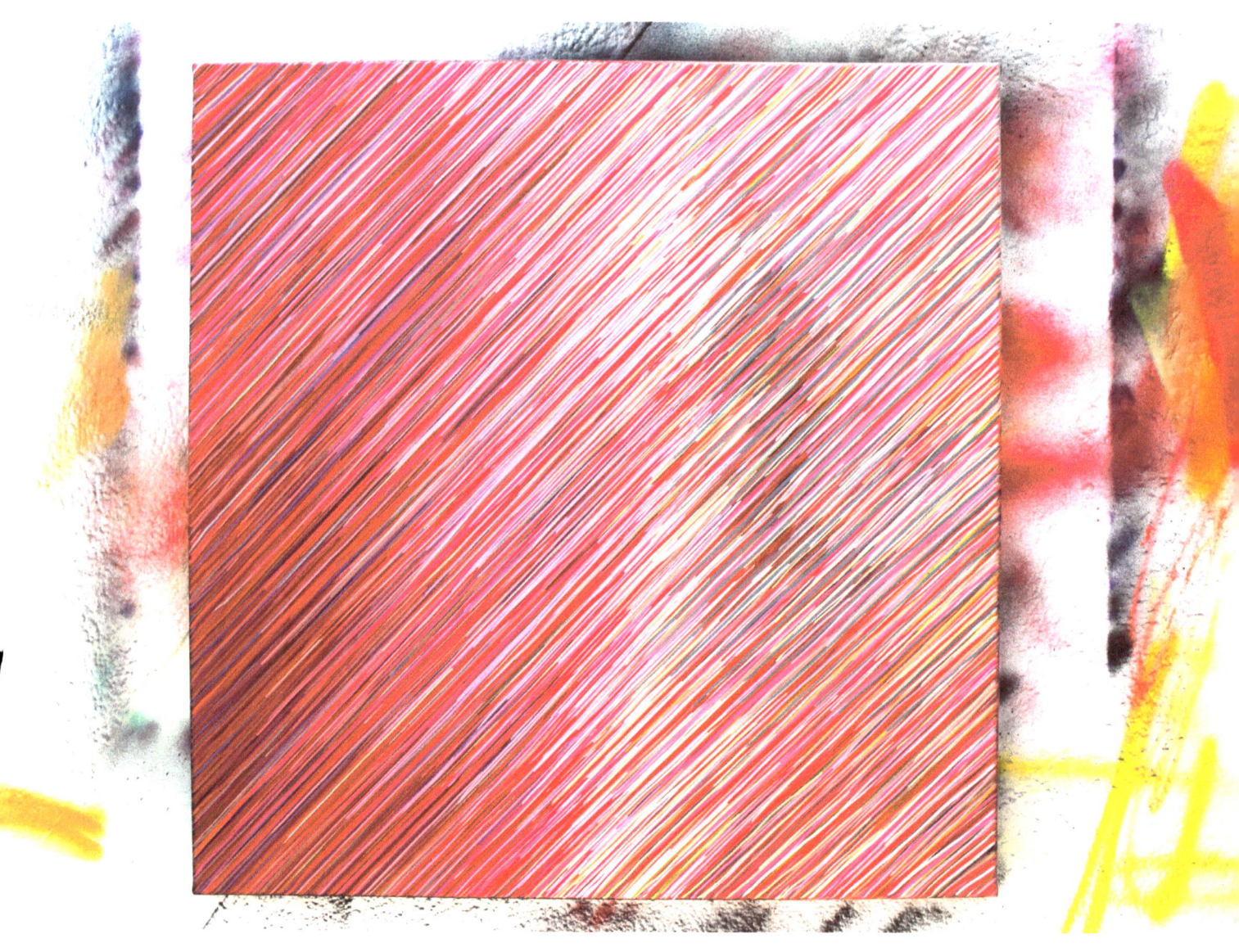

Overview:

As my art and vision evolve—from blank slate, to paper, to mural, to installation, to public space—I attempt to expand the viewer's understanding and comprehension of the spaces, structures, and communities around us. My intent is to integrate art into the existing environment, creating harmony, balance, and adding life to an otherwise colorless wall while also encouraging the viewer to consider space, culture and the larger world.

Construction:

Produced using a hatch drawing style, my work utilizes fine lines and details to create simultaneously diminutive constructions that, when viewed together, unfold as the viewer is physically positioned to the artwork- each stroke of color endowing the compositional elements with vibrancy and movement. Most of my work is figurative, and I draw inspiration from the surrounding community and content in the form and expression of my subjects. More recently I have explored the connection of the existing architecture and construction of the physical buildings to the work itself. Natural surfaces and extant flaws, such as inset holes and missing bricks, become desirable parts of the canvas.

Theme Relative to Project:

Throughout my travels to Israel, Russia, Hong Kong, Mexico, Malaysia, Japan, the United States and Europe, I have explored the social construct of individual versus community in my work. Diverse cultures and heritages interest me and I create work as a catalyst for discussing diversity and community. In recognition of an inherent interconnectedness of the individual within the community, many of my recent murals have featured individuals that are distinct from the surrounding community – resulting in an intermingling of cultures within the space where the piece is based. The facture of my paintings echo this theme with each tiny line, communicating the innate relationship between individual within the larger composition of community.

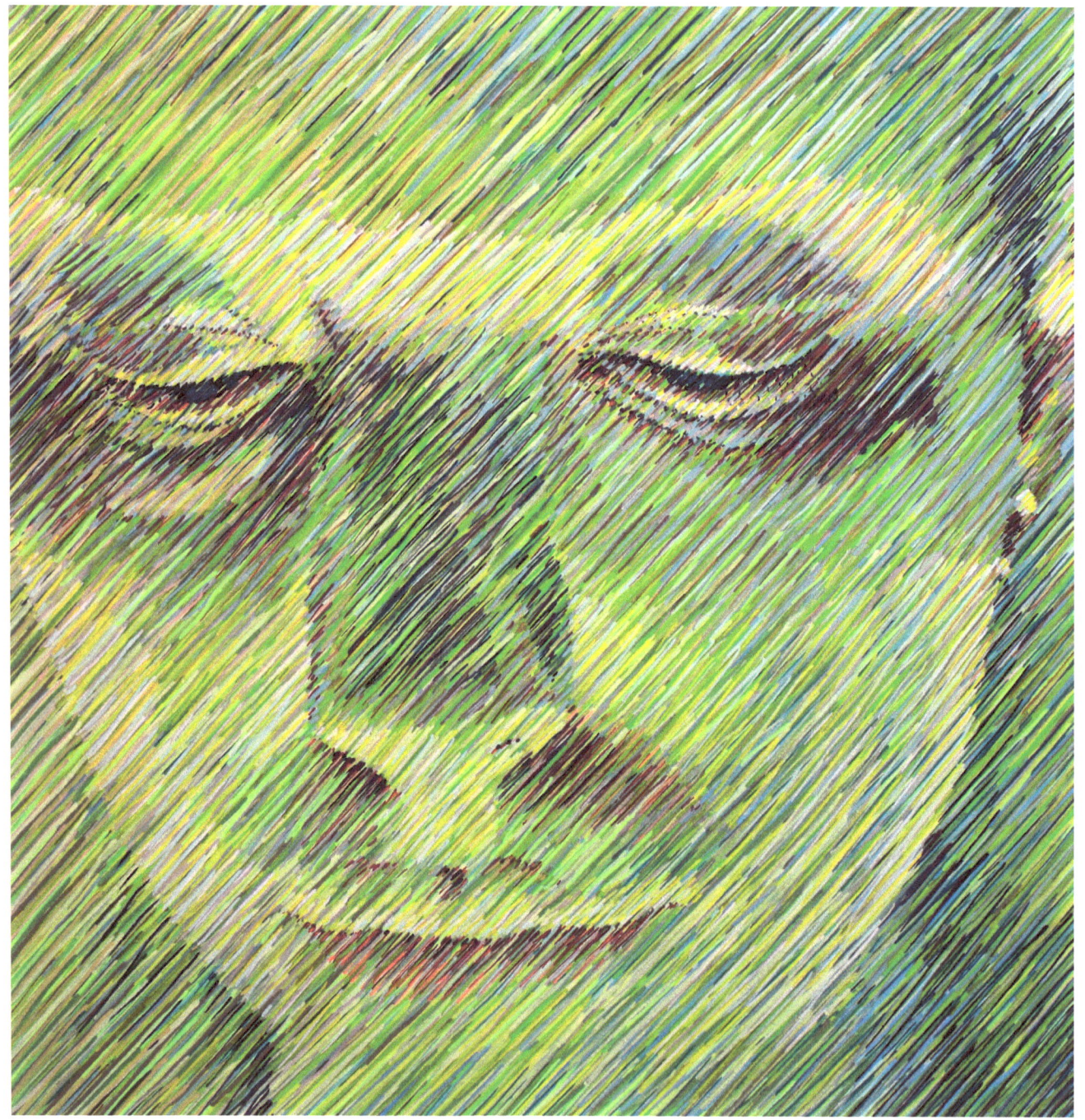

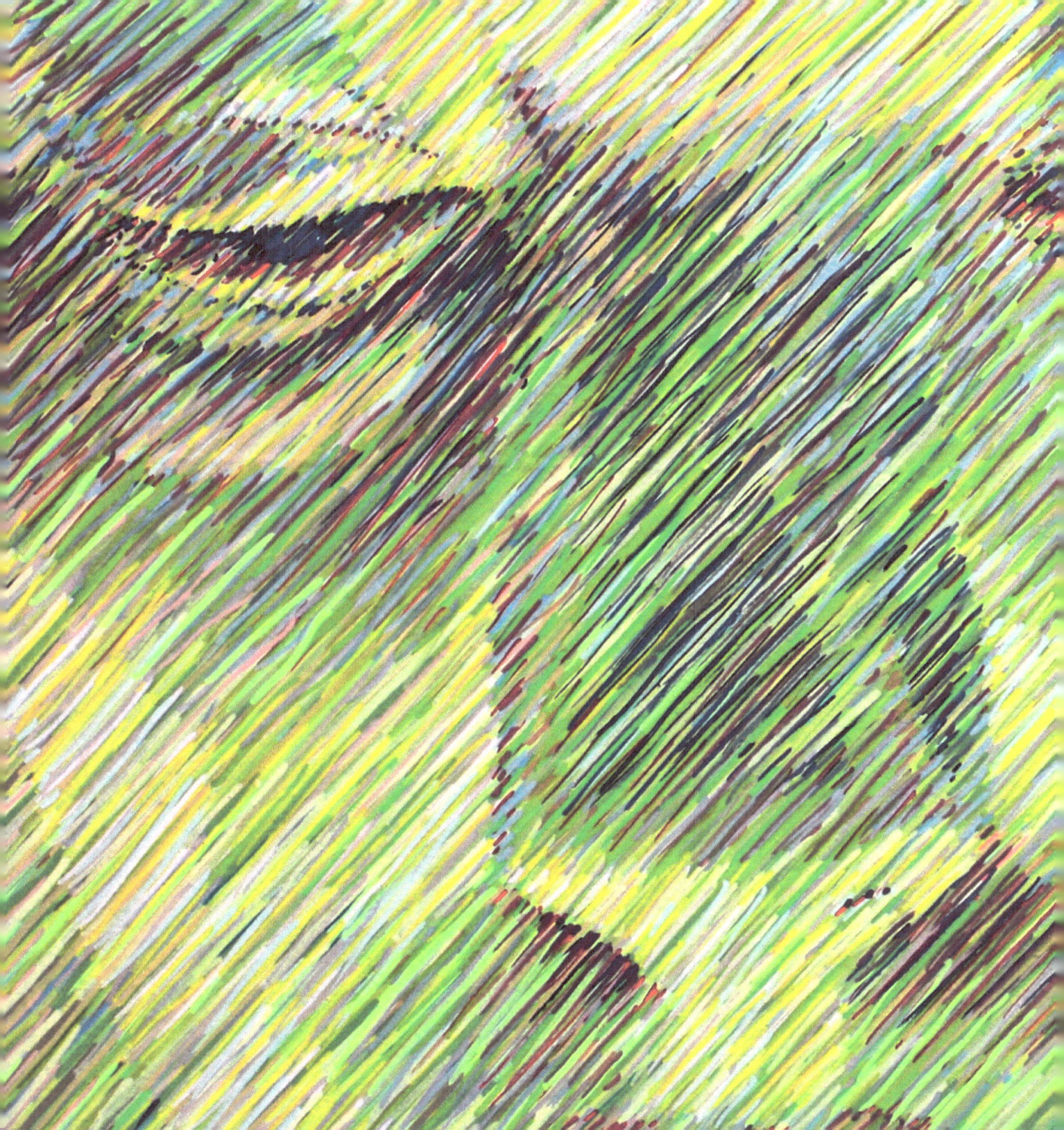

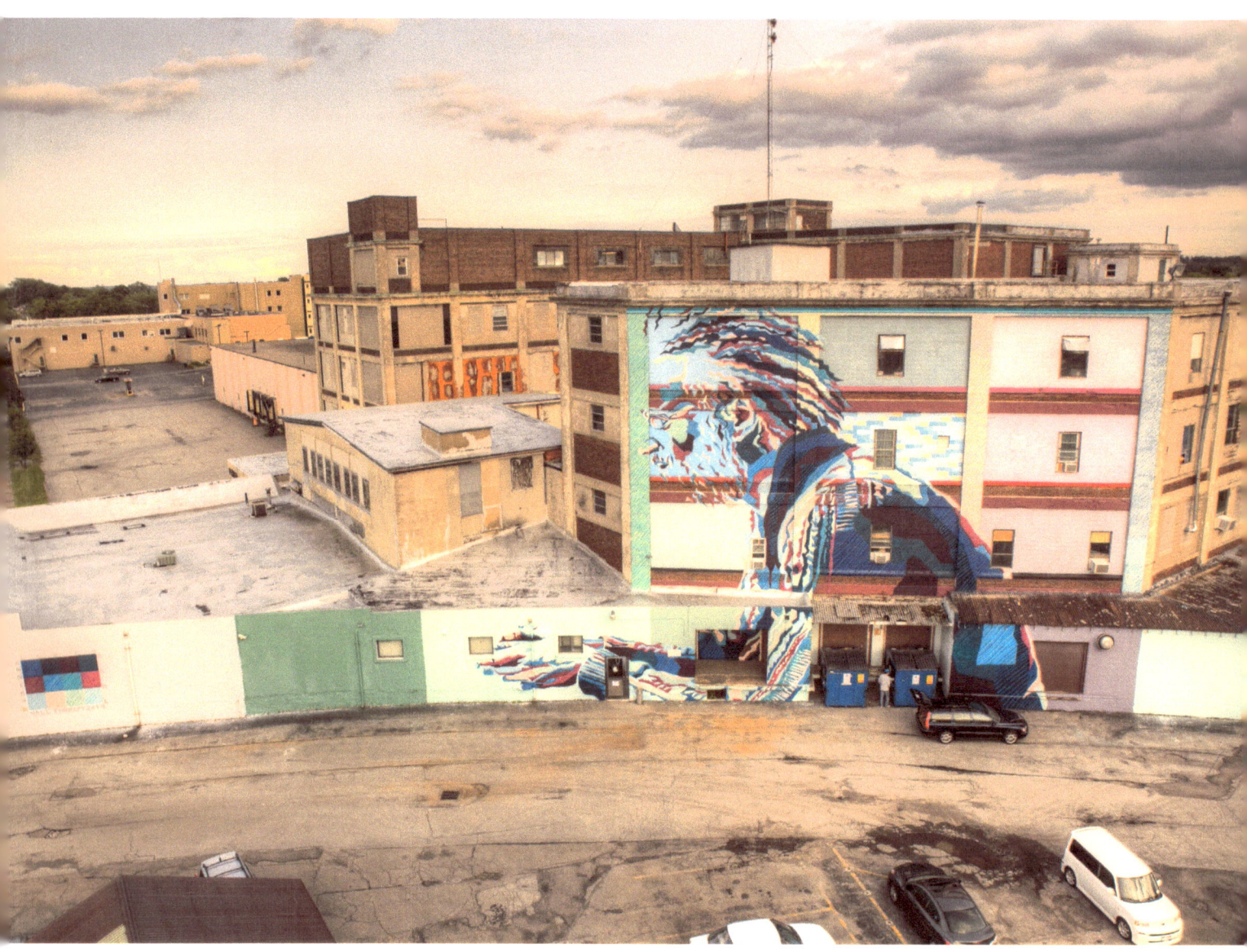

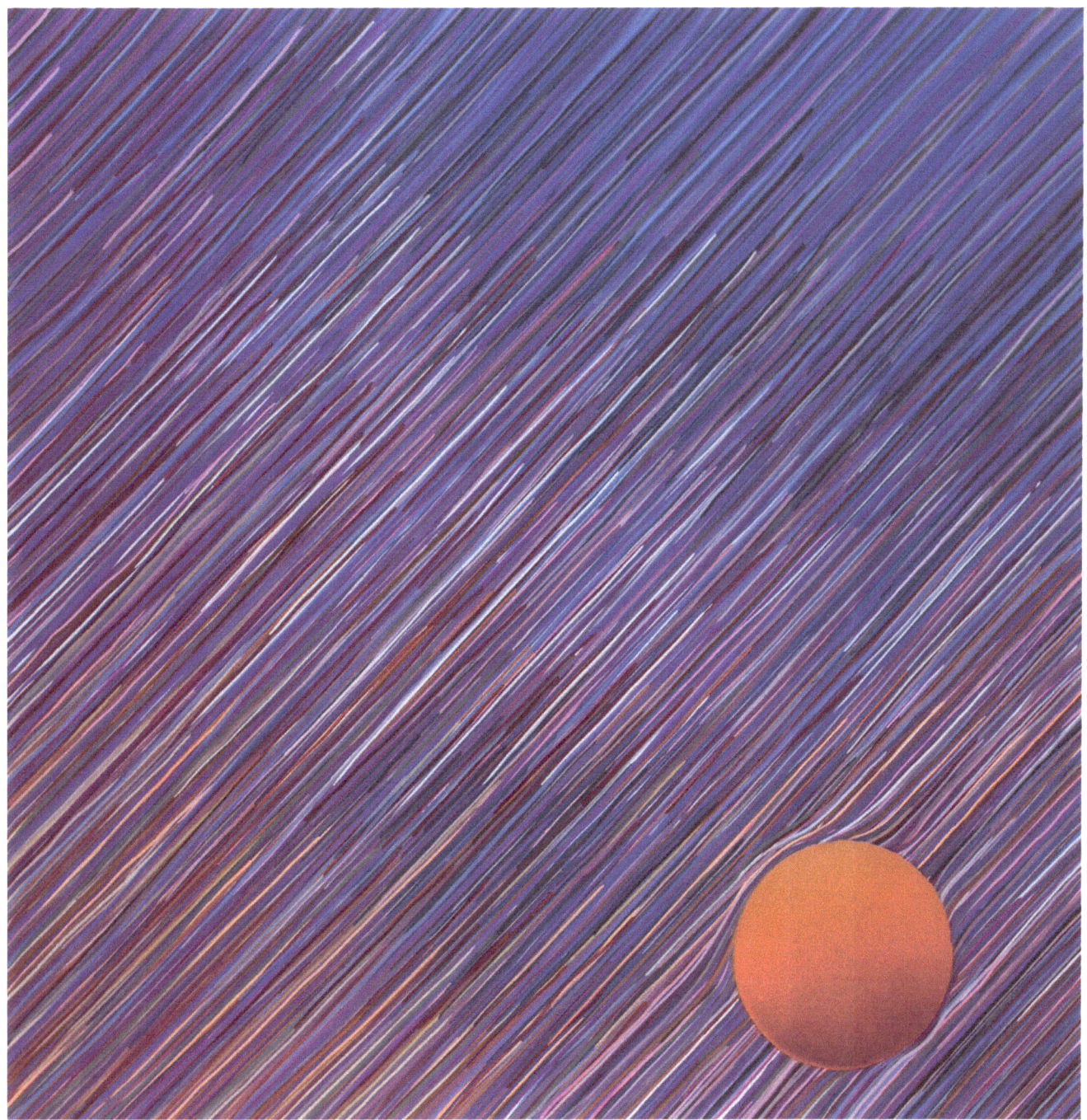

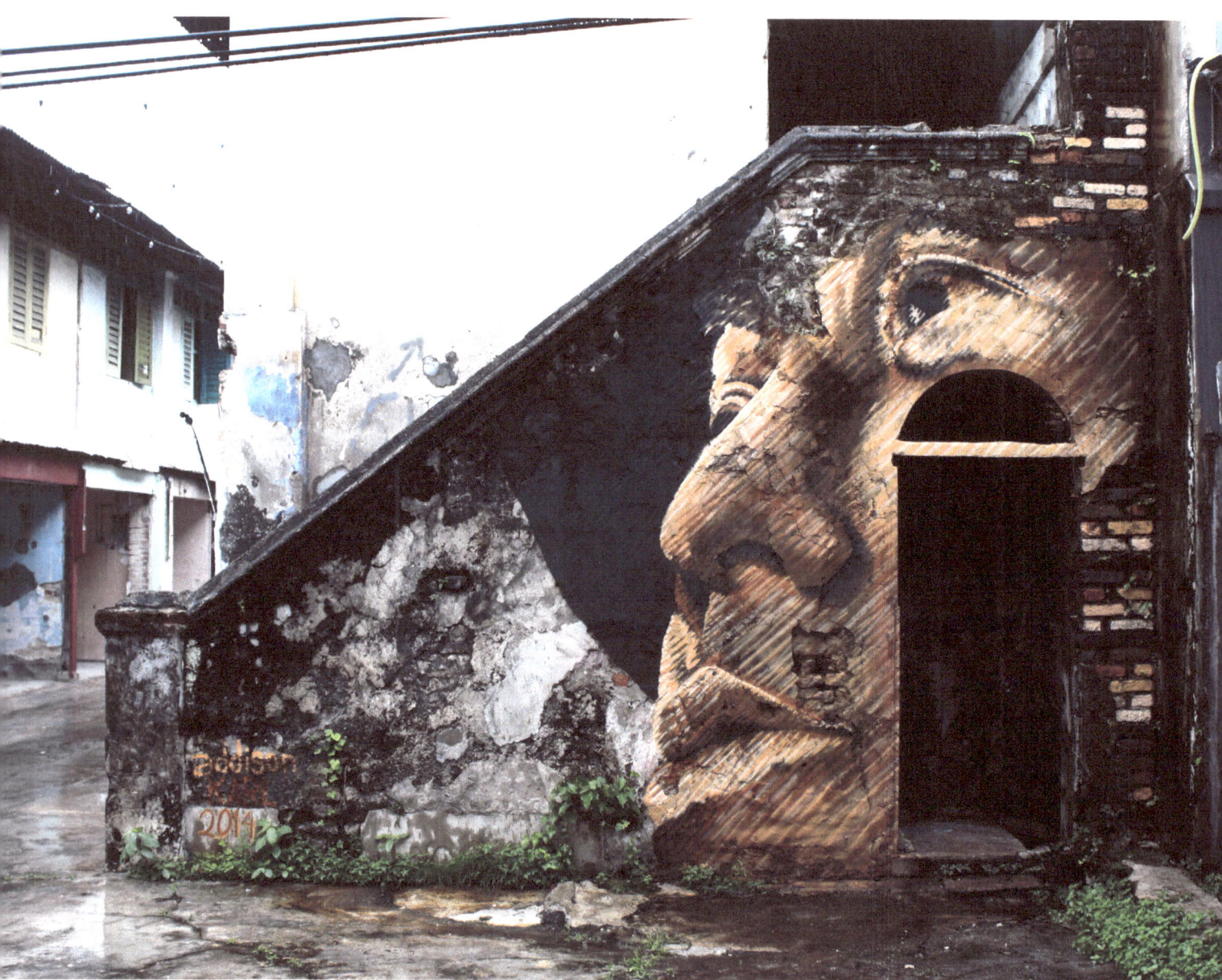

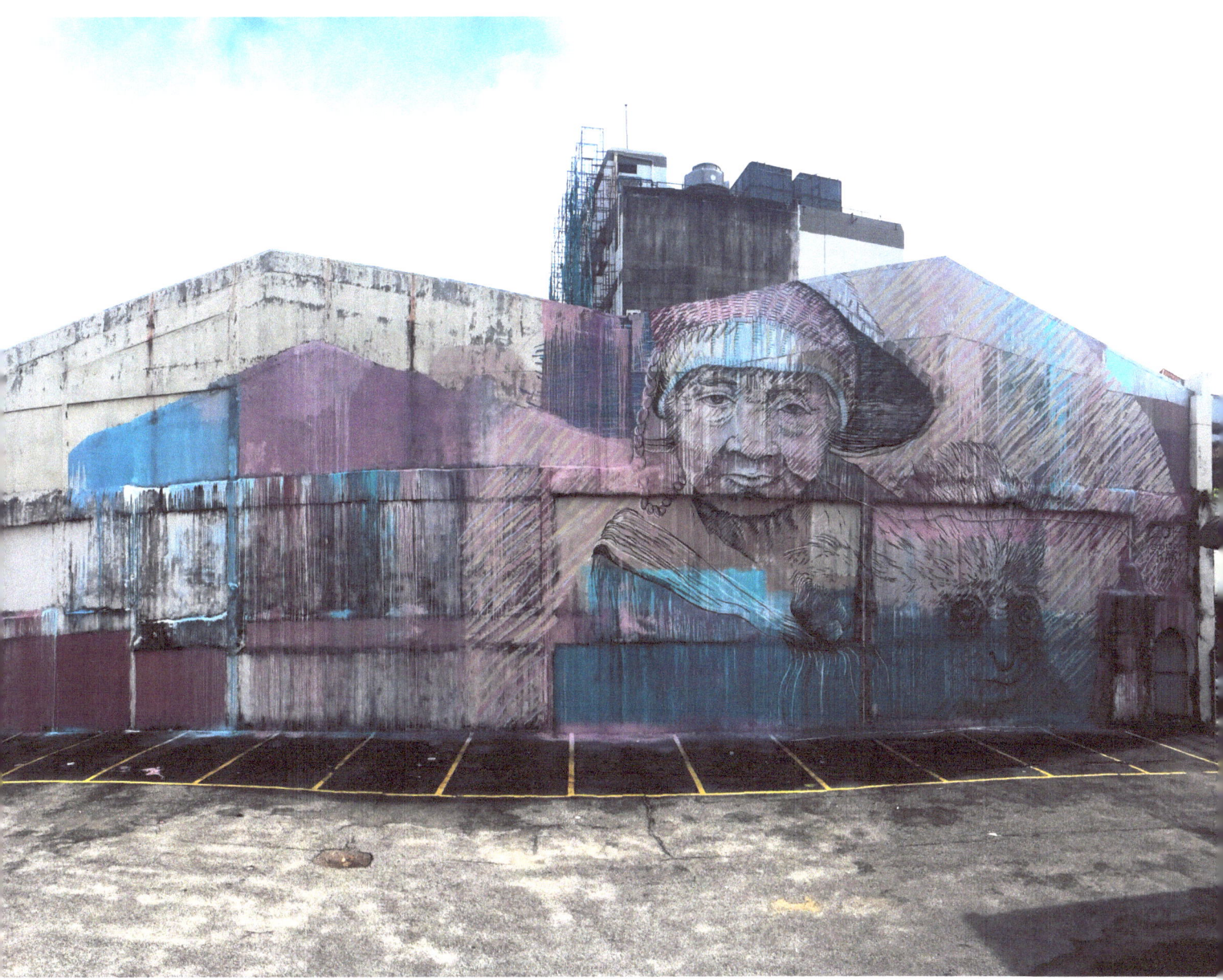

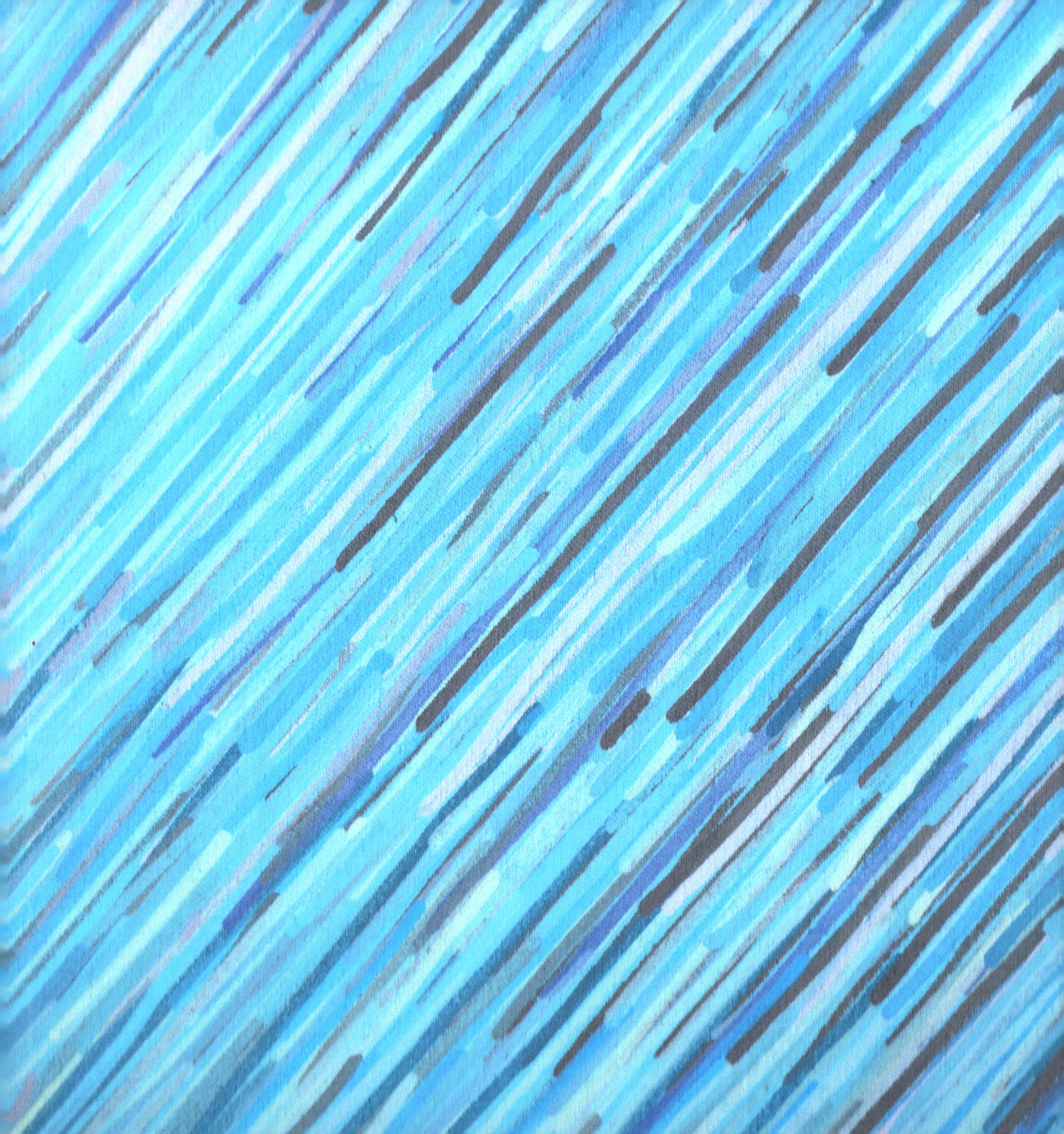

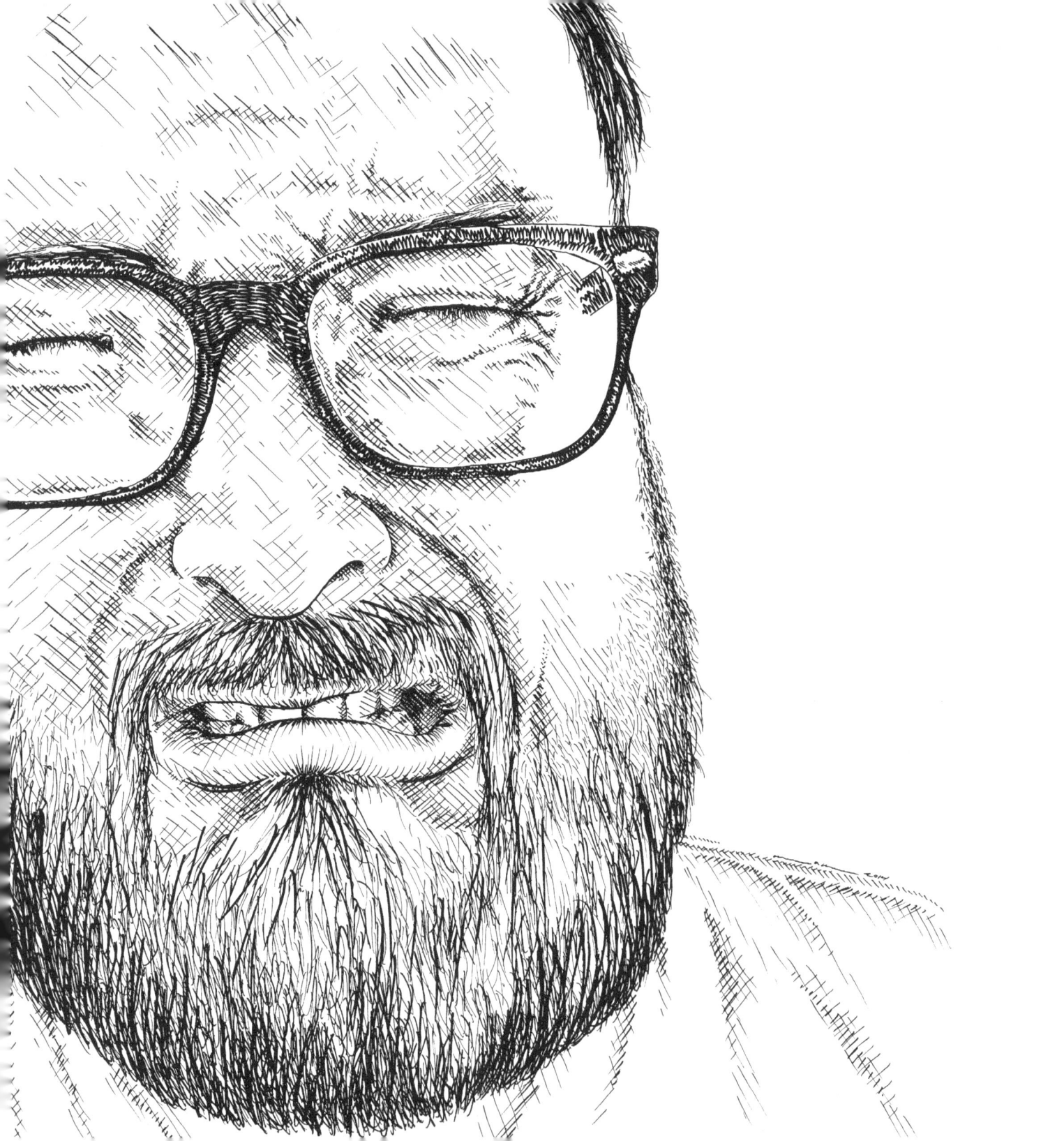

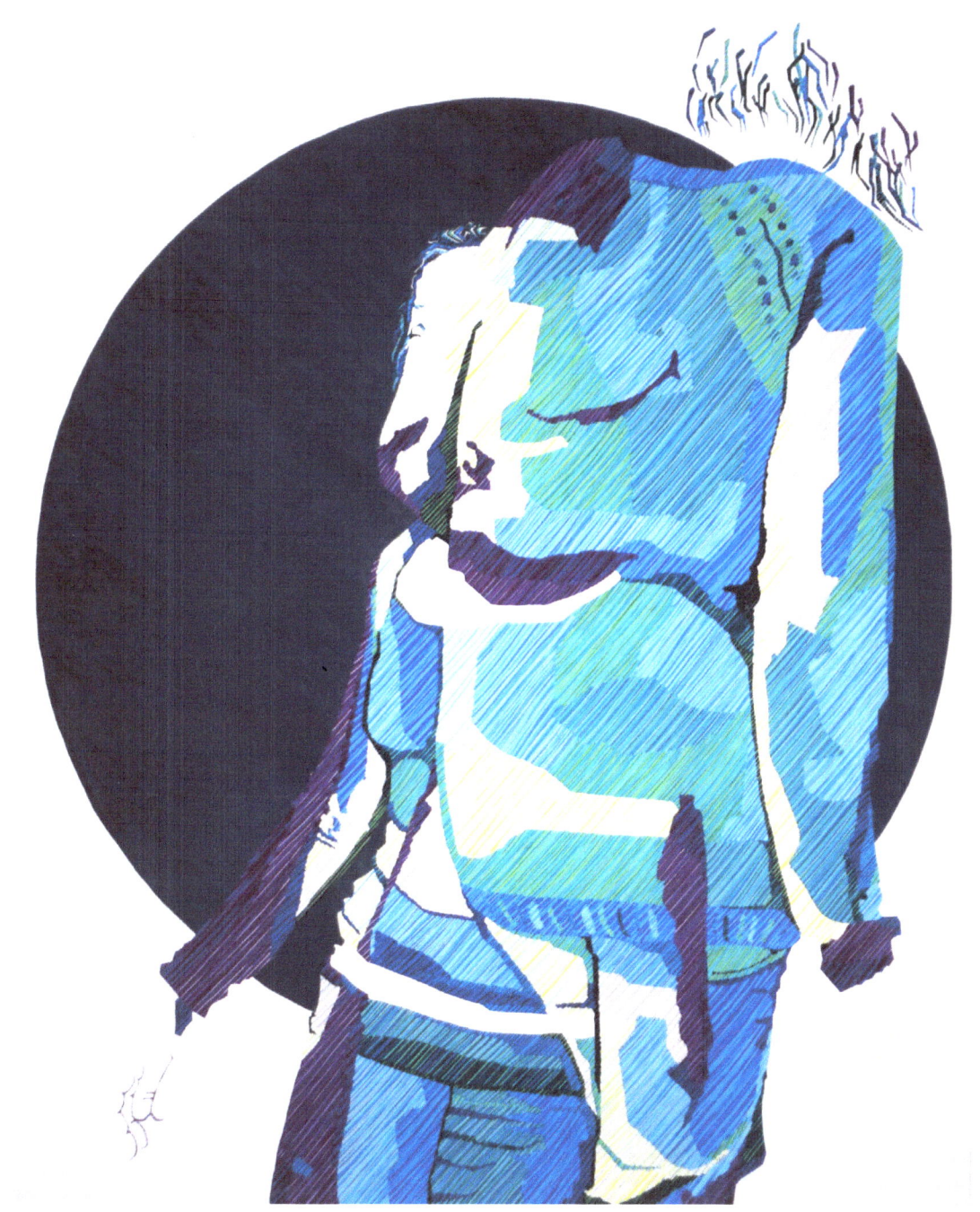

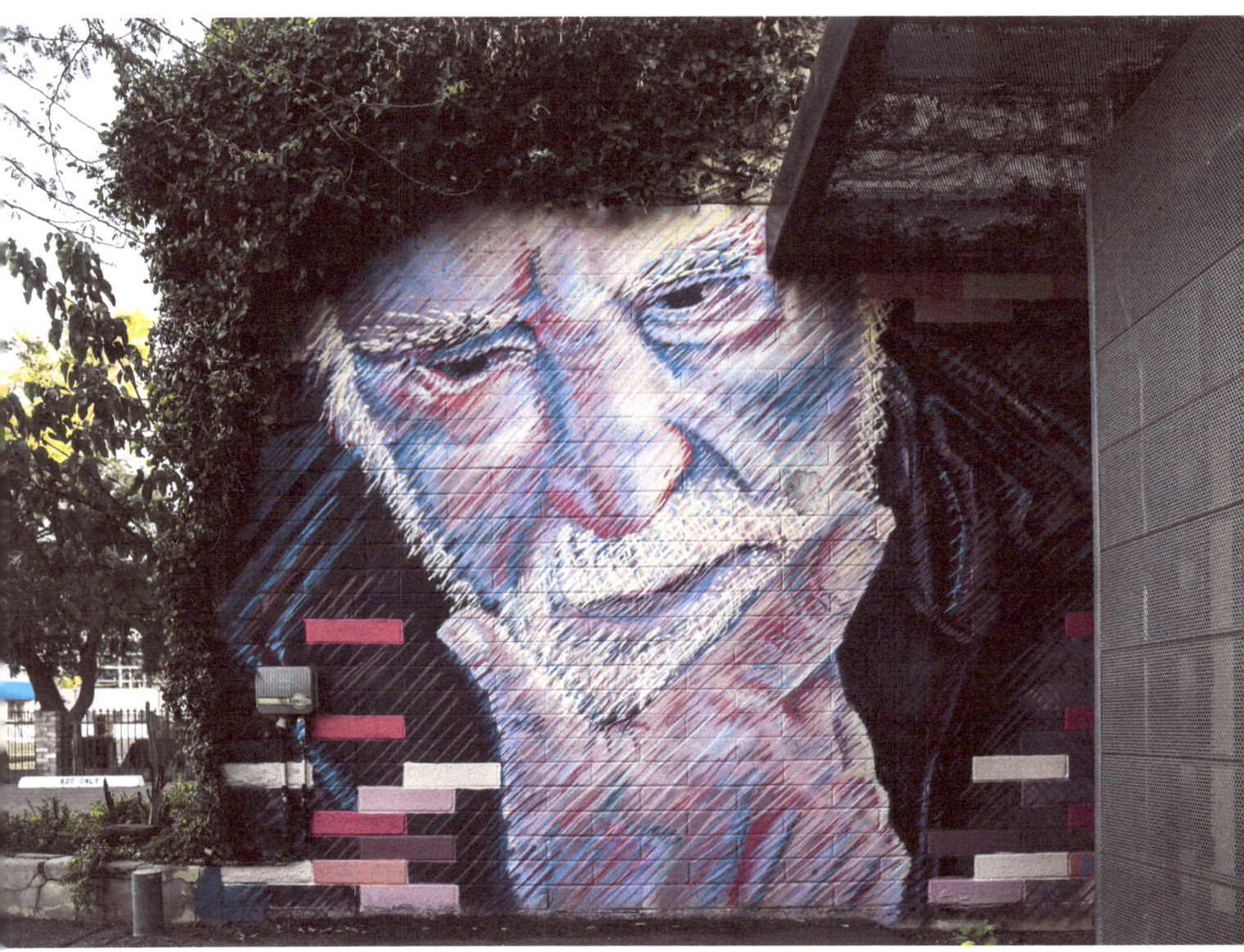

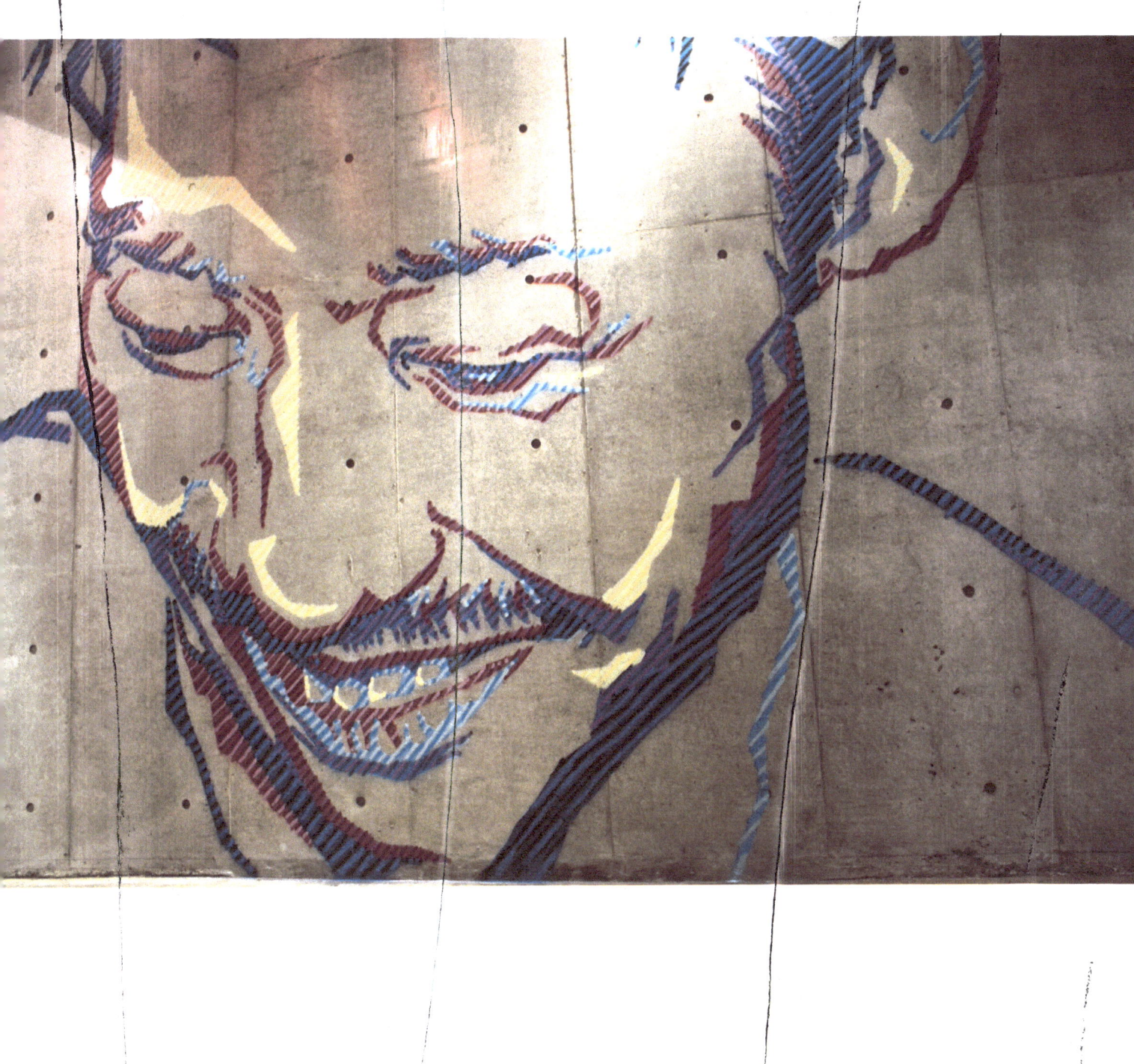

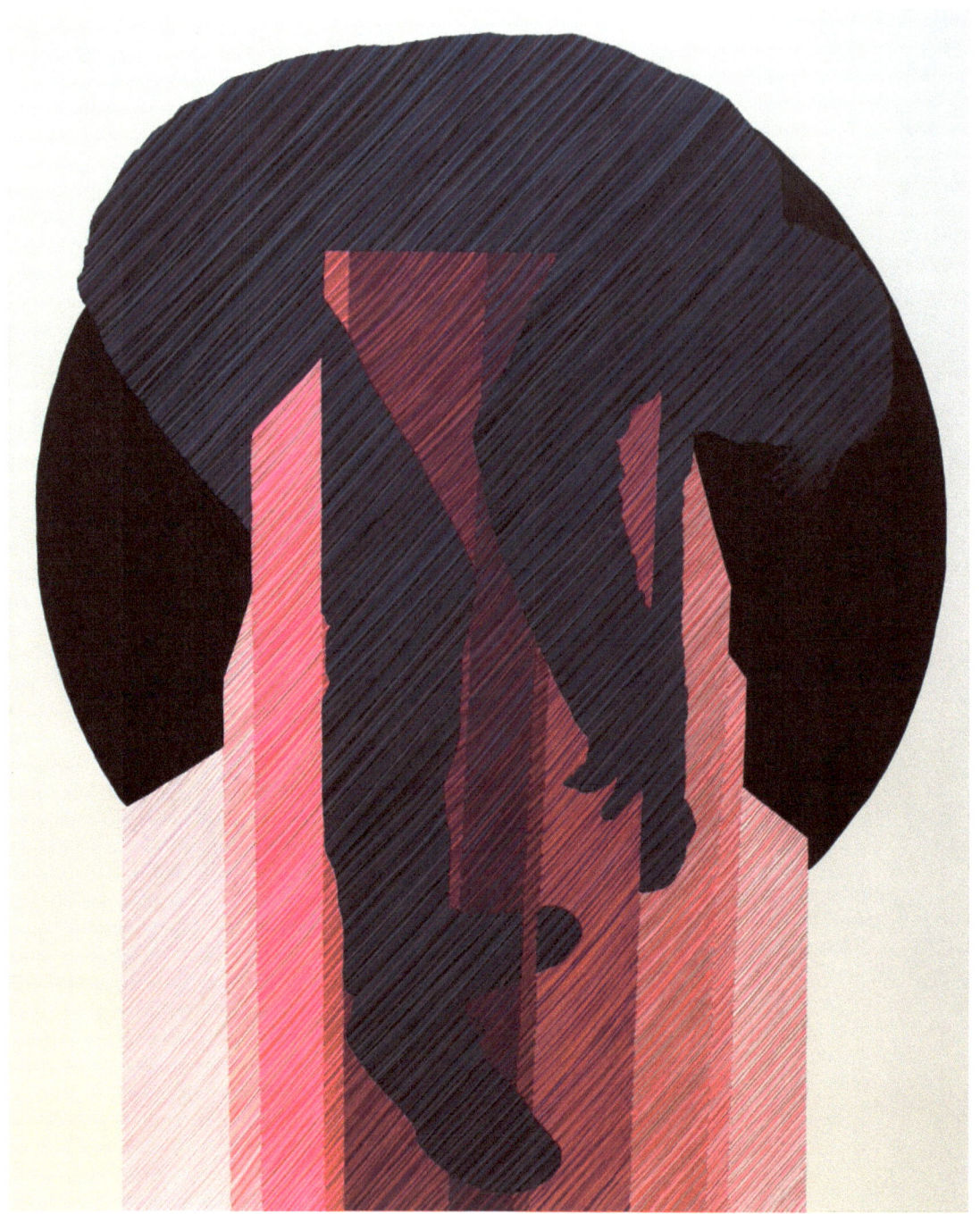

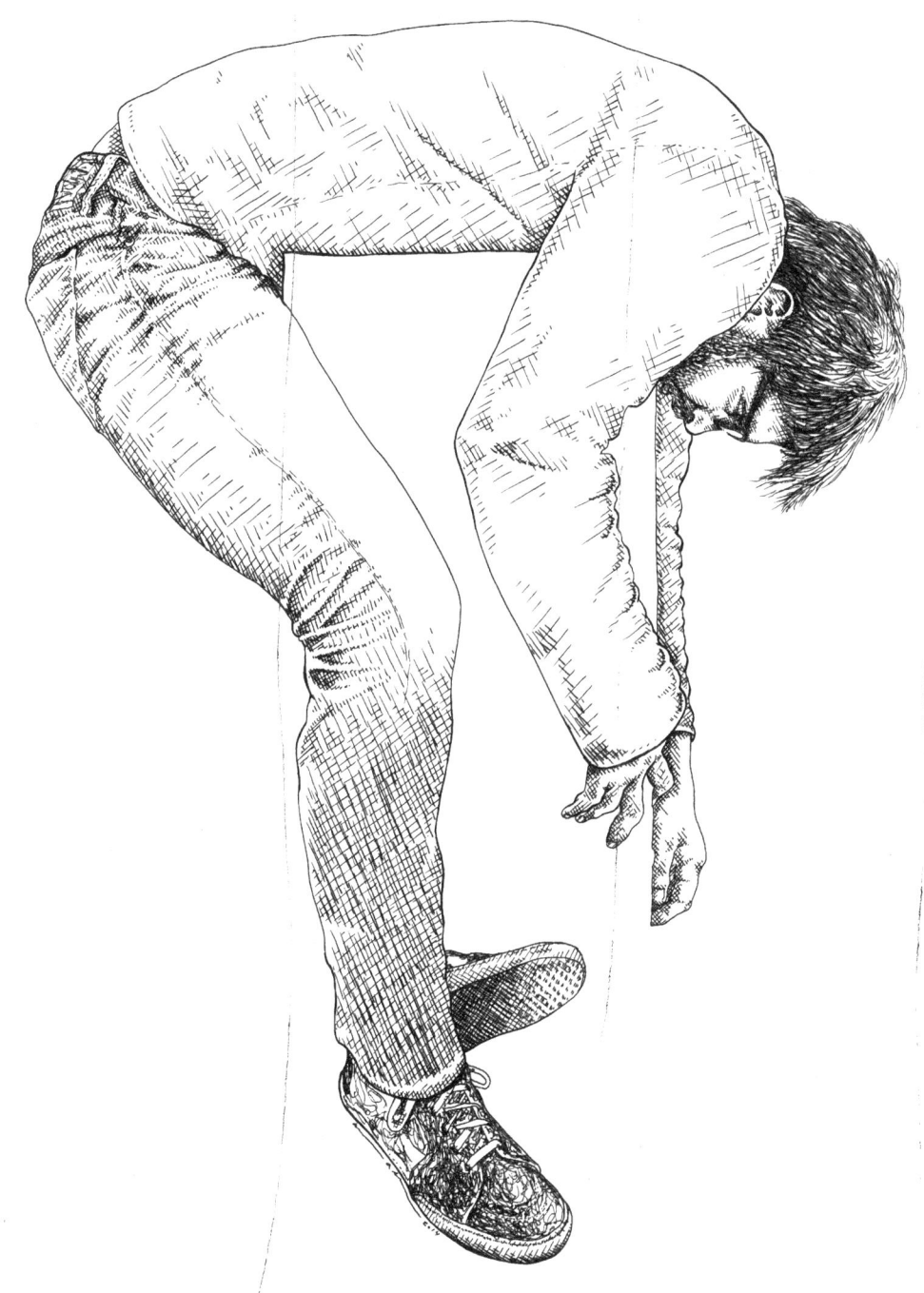

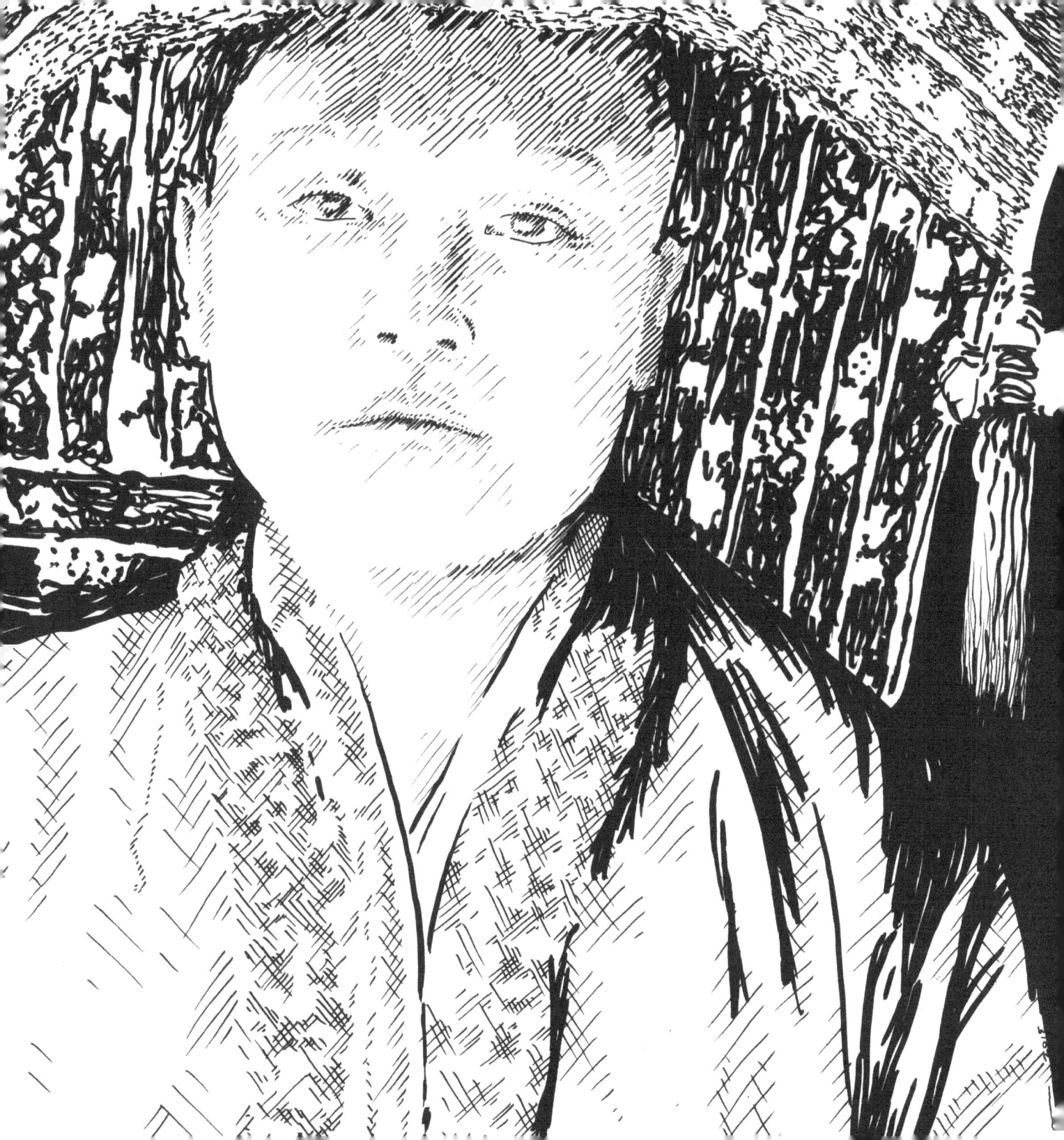

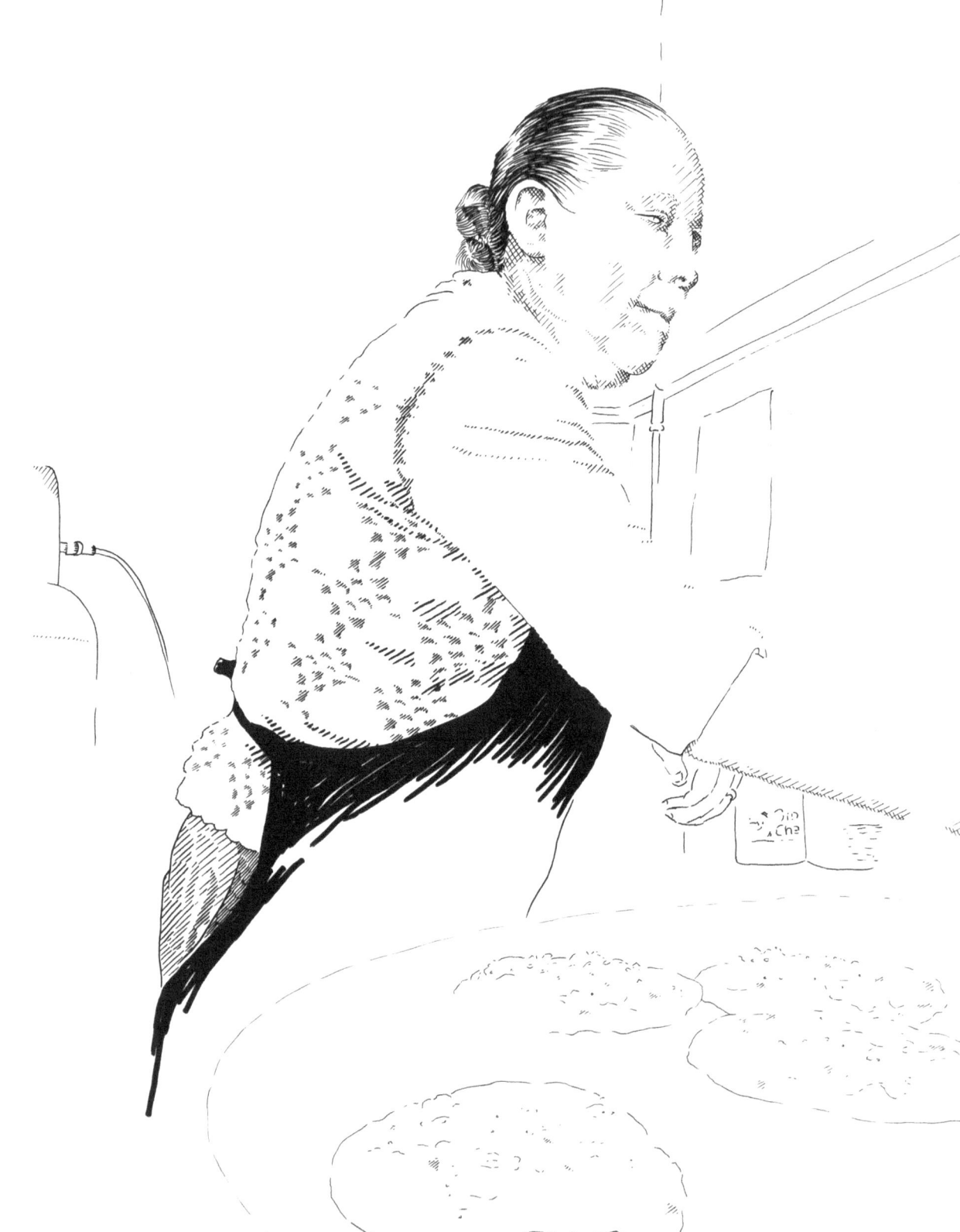

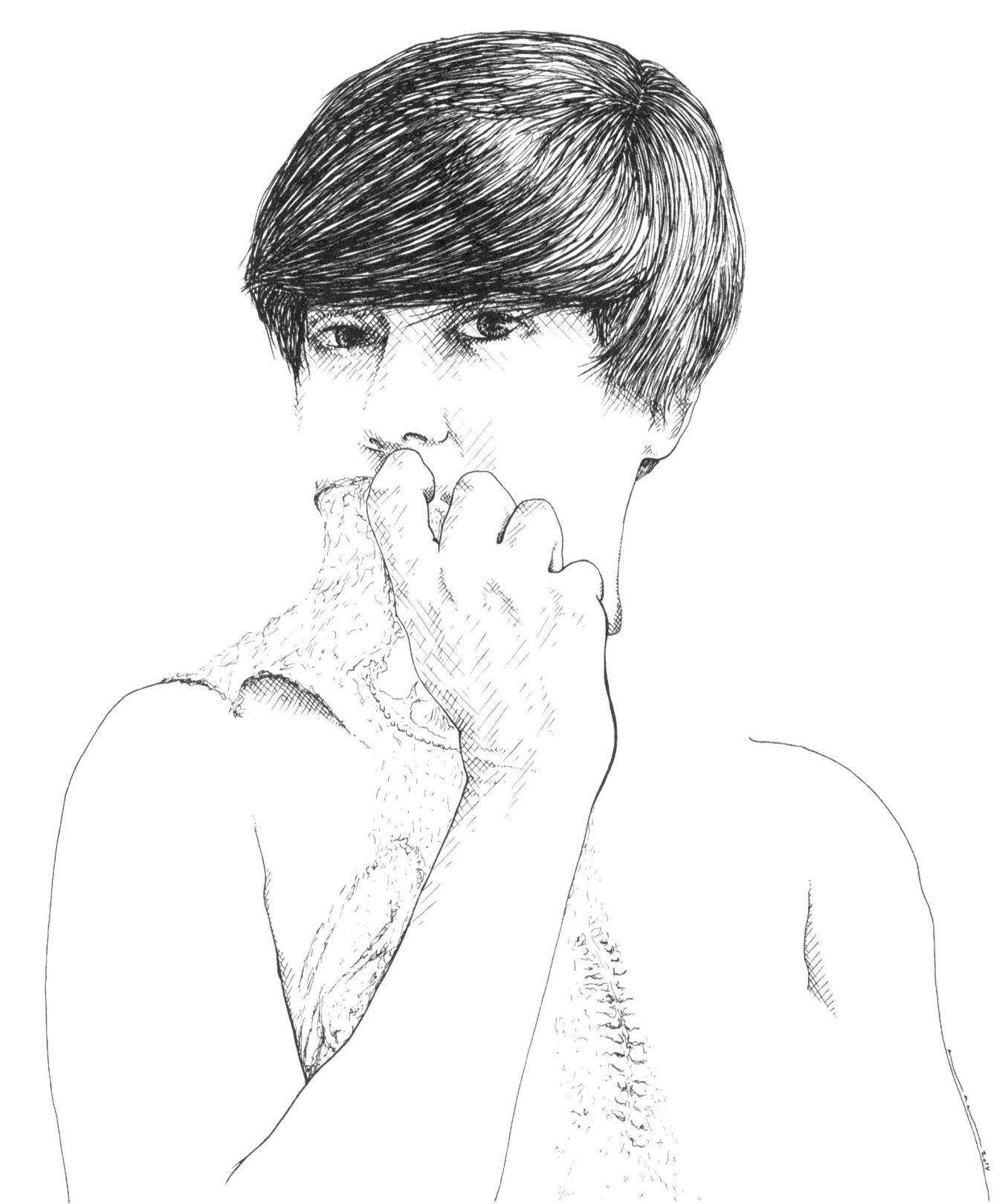

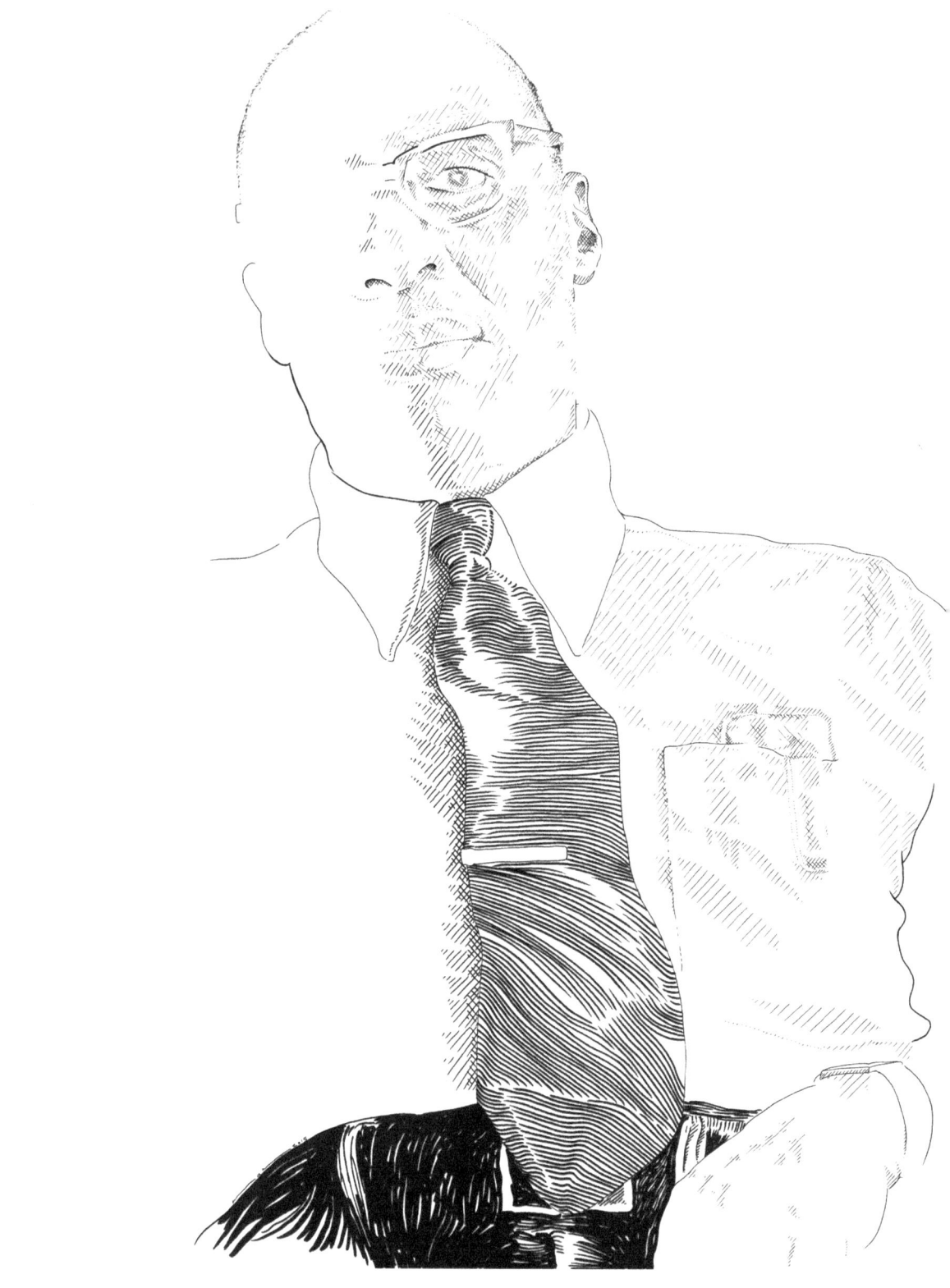

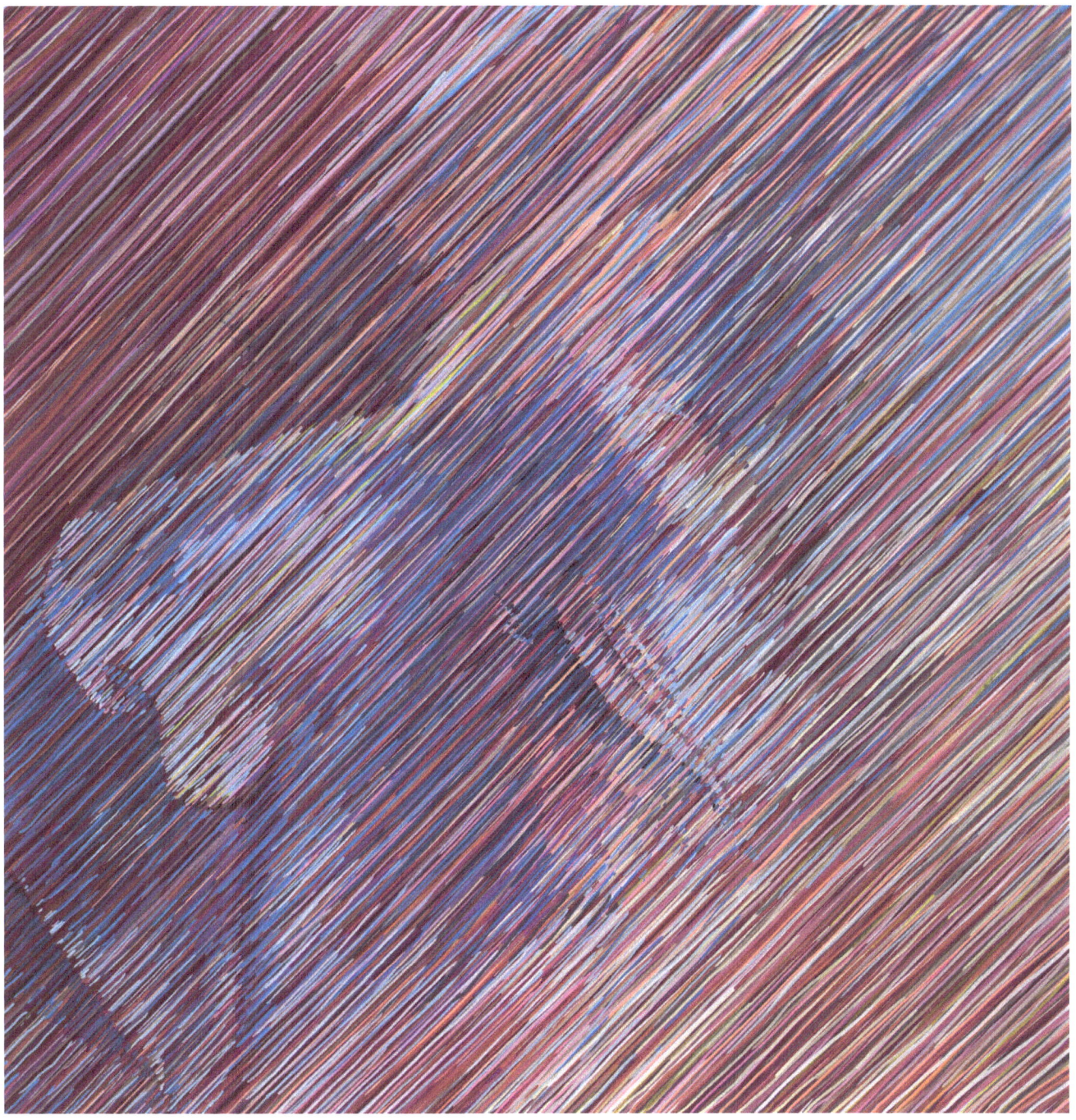

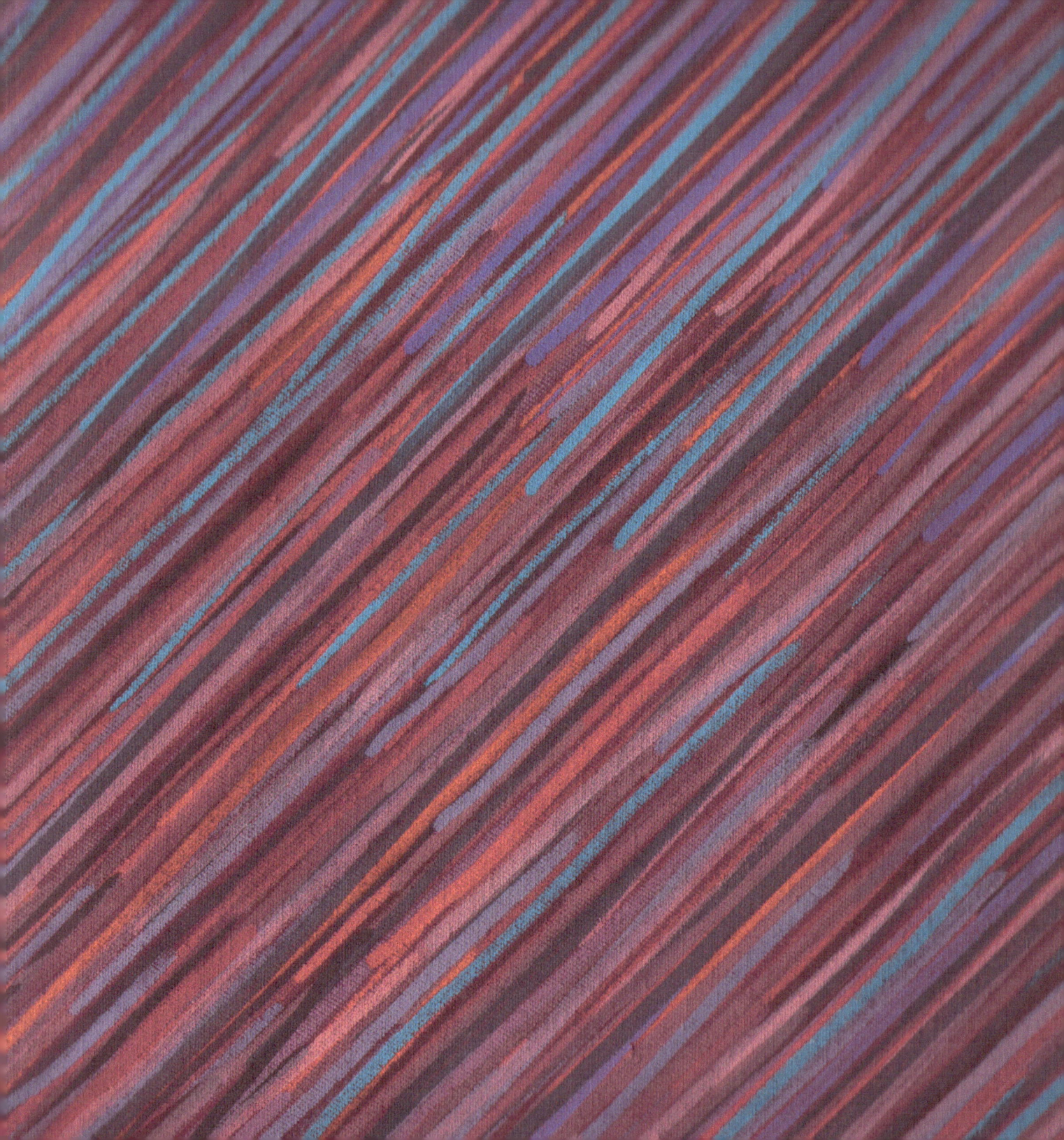

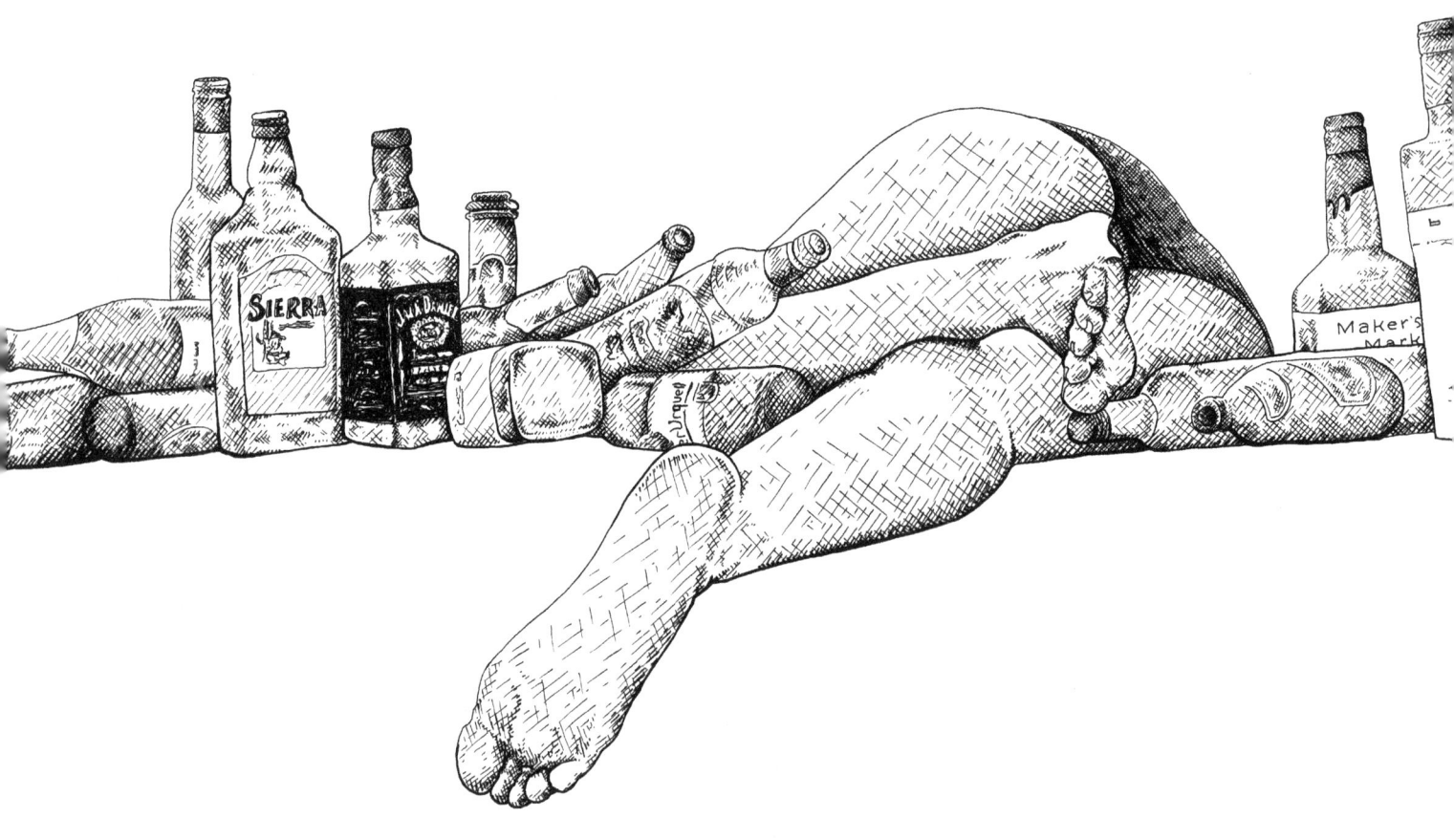

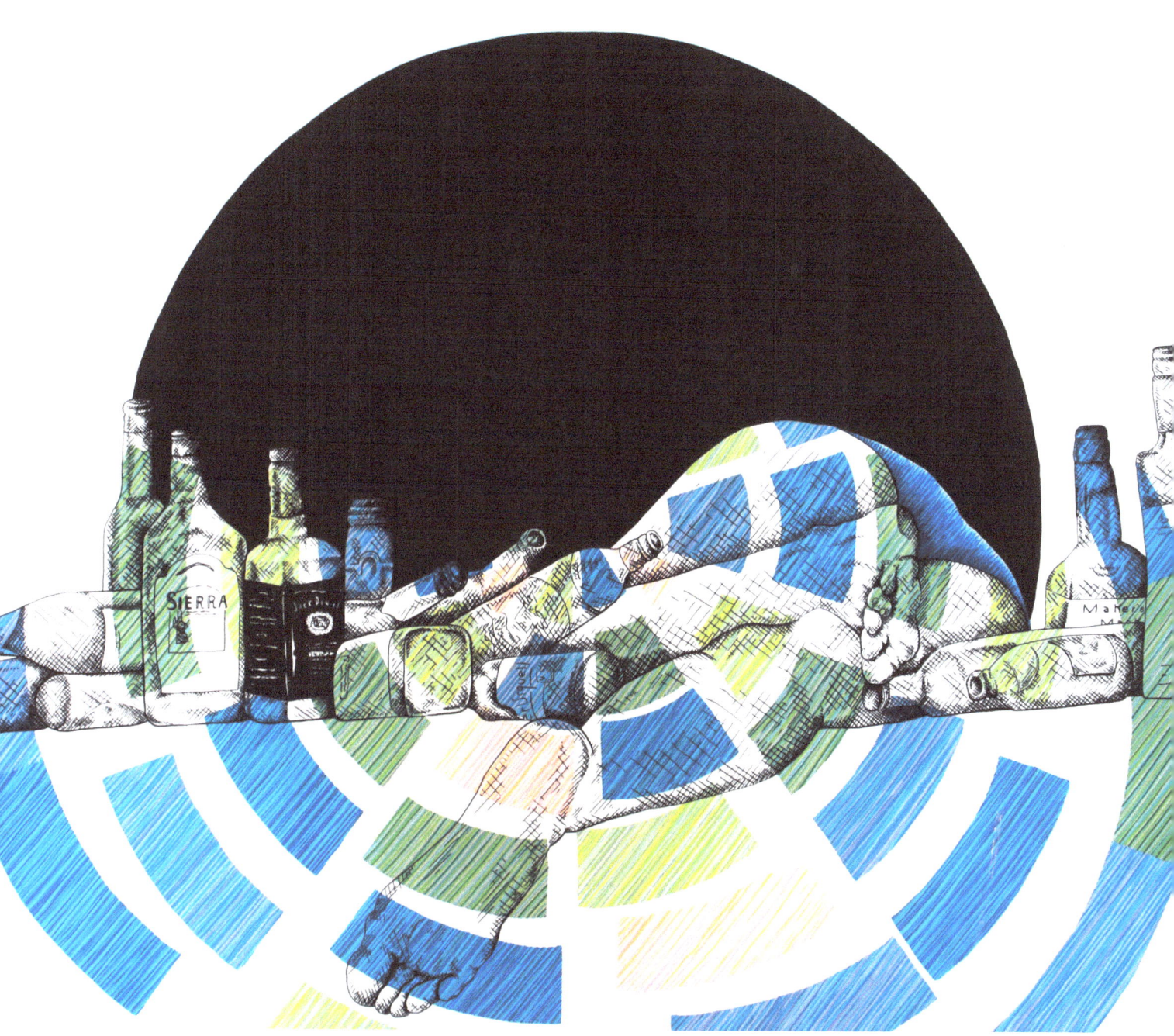

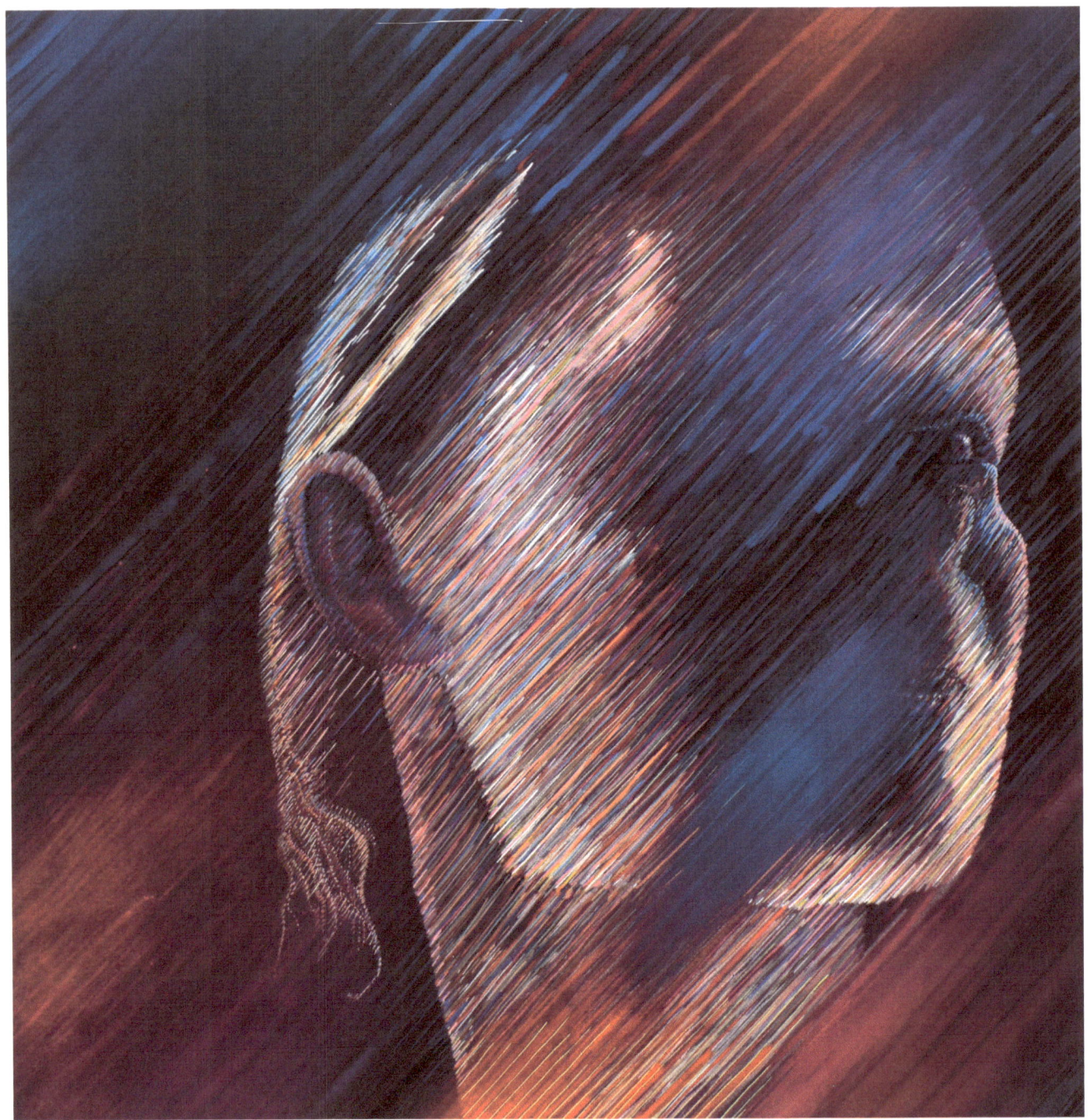

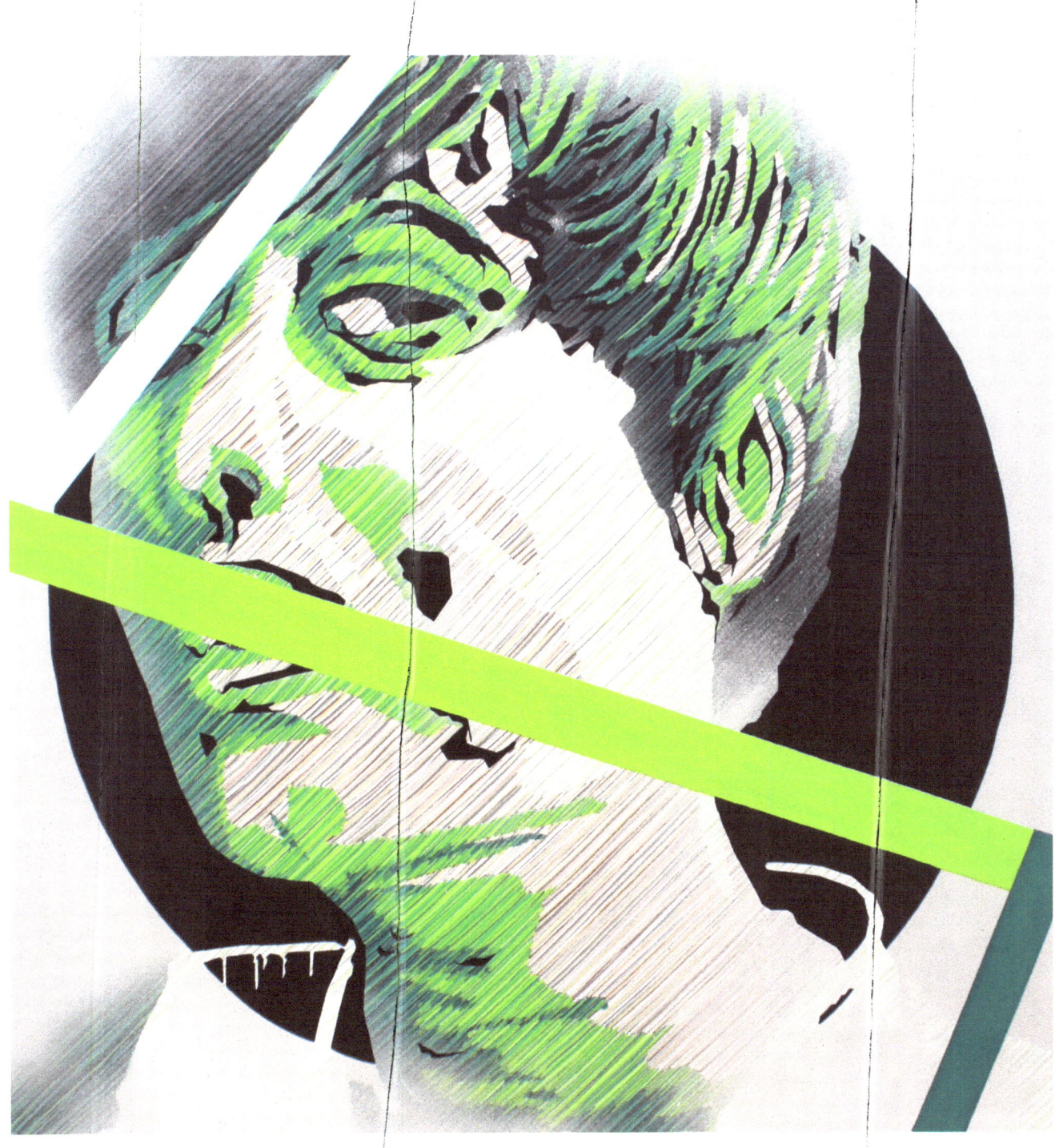

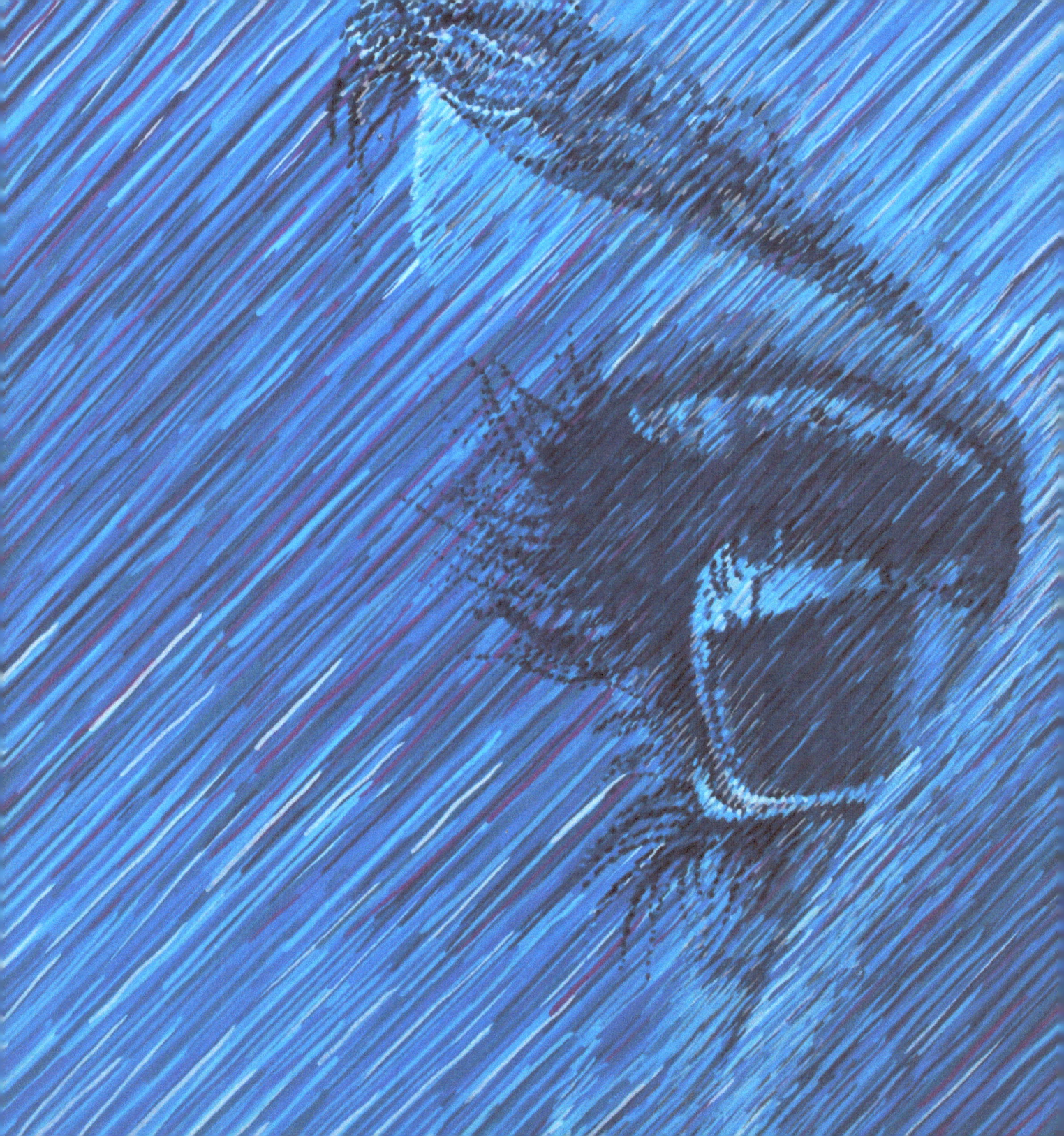

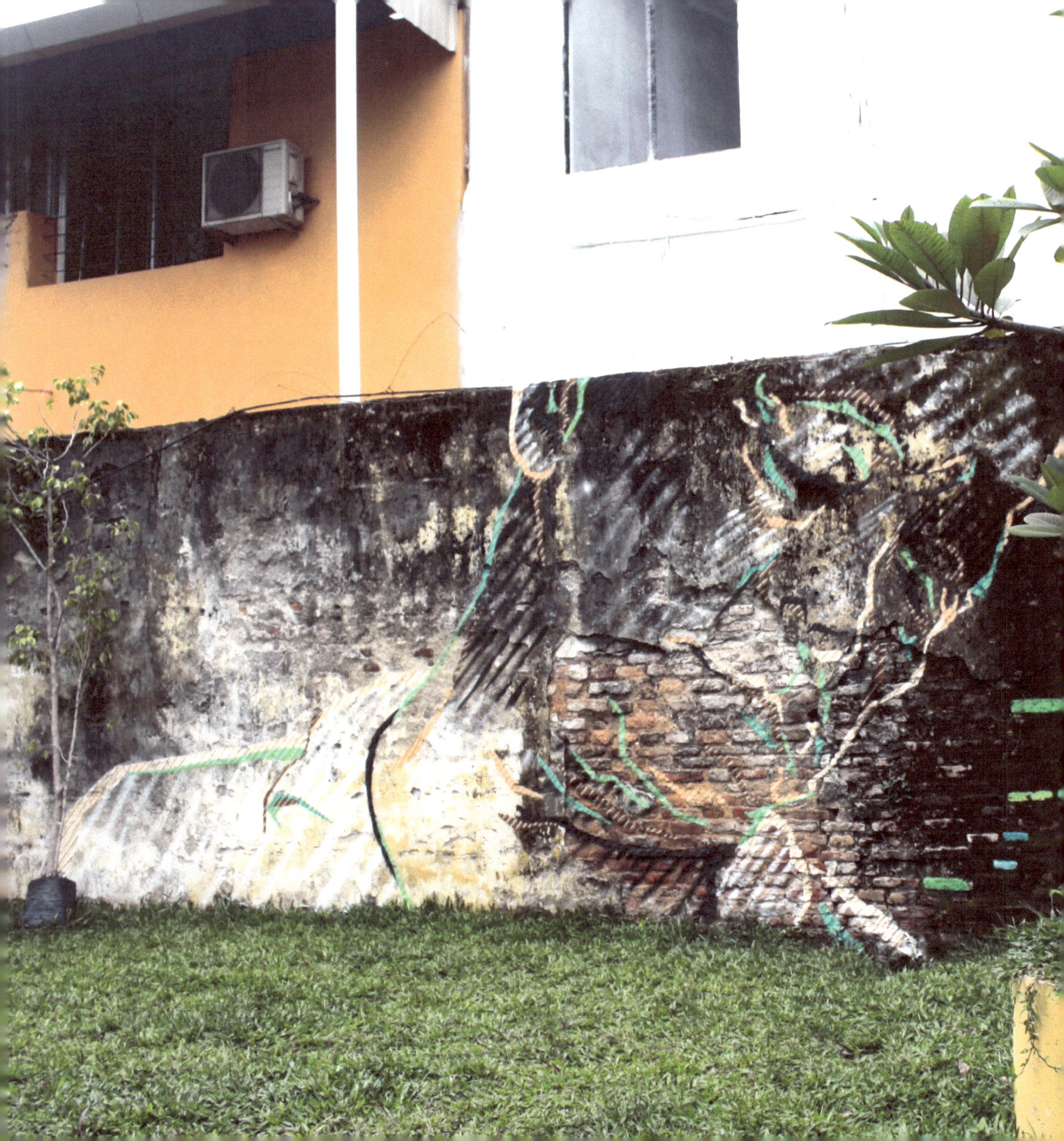

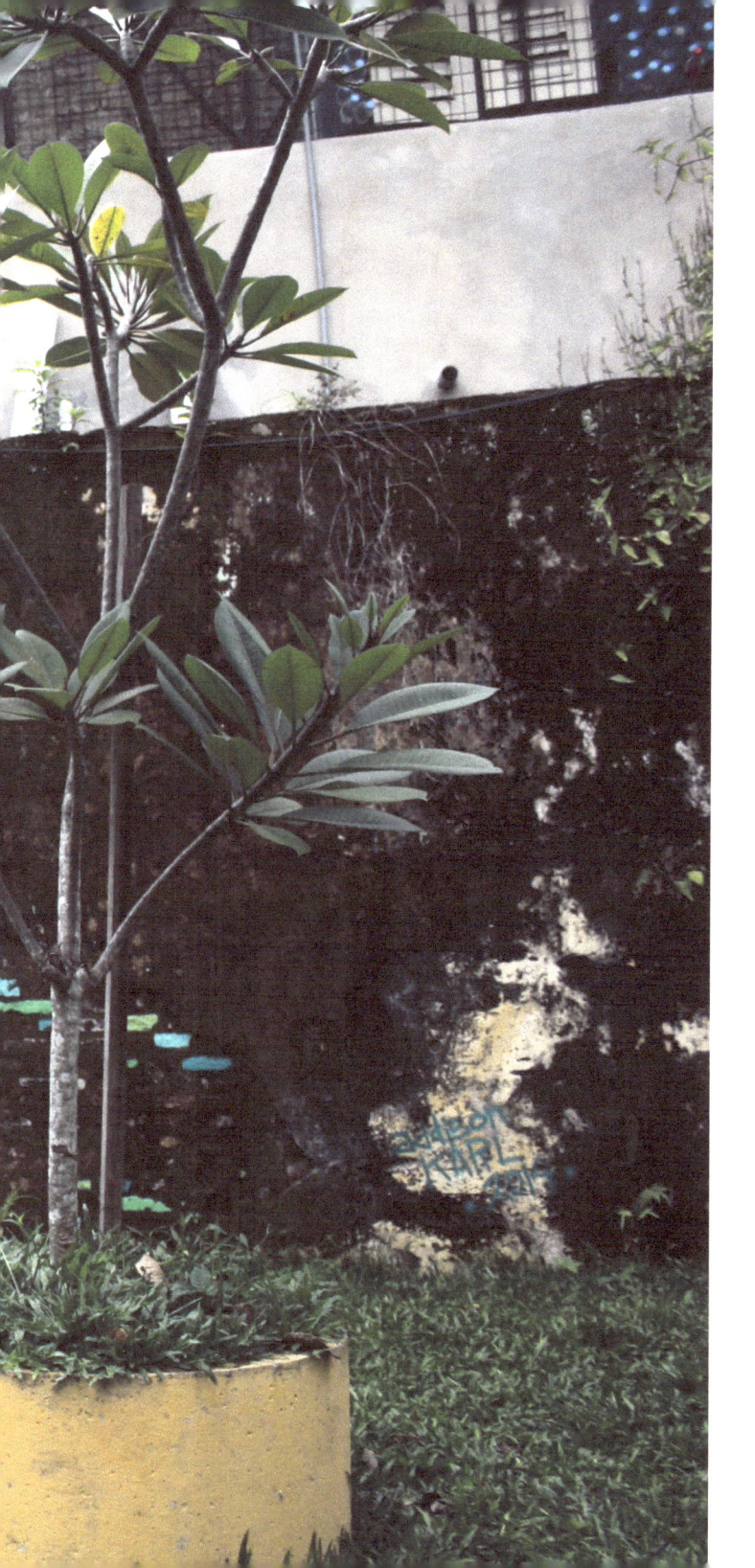

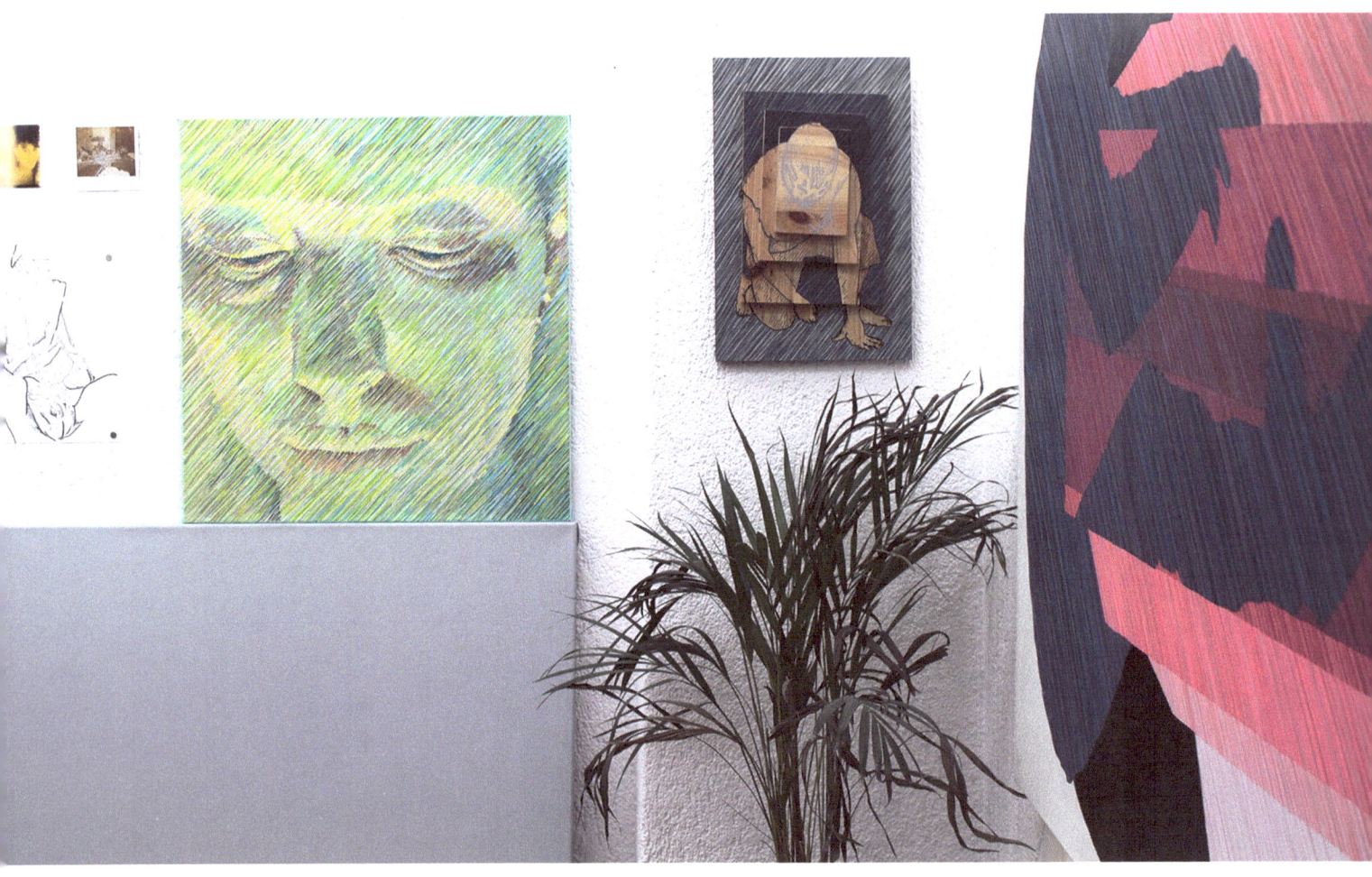

<< Artwork By Addison Karl >>

All content © 2015 and Published by Karl Addison - 4610 Marine View Pl. Bremerton, WA 98312

Title: Polaris - Author: Addison Karl - Publisher: Karl Addison - Address: 4610 Marine View Pl. Bremerton, WA 98312 - Format: Paperback - Publication Date: August 2015 - ISBN: 978-1517010096

<< Index >>

www.ingramcontent.com/pod-product-compliance
Lightning Source LLC
Chambersburg PA
CBHW050904180526
45159CB00007B/2791